passport to academic presentations

Student's Book

Douglas Bell

COVENTRY UNIVERTY LONDON
University House
109 - 117 Middlesex Street, London, E1 7JF
Tel: 024 7765 1016
www.coventry.ac.uk/london

Garnet
EDUCATION

Published by

Garnet Publishing Ltd.
8 Southern Court
South Street
Reading RG1 4QS, UK

2nd edition published 2014.
Reprinted 2015, 2016, 2017.

ISBN 978-1-90861-468-1
British Cataloguing-in-Publication Data
A catalogue record for this book is available from the British Library.

Production

Project manager:	Richard Peacock
Editorial team:	Emily Clarke, Fiona McGarry
Design:	Neil Collier, Mike Hinks
Illustration:	Doug Nash
Photography:	Clipart.com, Getty Images, Corbis images, iStockphoto, Shutterstock
Audio production:	WEP UK Productions

Acknowledgements

The author and publisher wish to thank the following for permission to use or adapt their
material for use in *Passport to Academic Presentations*:

Page 7, photograph of Philip Larkin, taken by Jane Brown, reproduced with kind permission of
The Guardian newspaper. Copyright © Guardian News & Media Ltd 2003.
Page 13, History and Development of Paper text, reproduced with kind permission of Kew Gardens.
Page 44, Saving tips for students text © 2007 Karen Schweitzer. Used with permission of About
Inc., which can be found online at www.about.com. All rights reserved.
Page 58, Averting a water crisis text, reproduced with kind permission of the International Food
Policy Research Institute www.ifpri.org. This press release can be found online at
http://www.ifpri.org/sites/default/files/pubs/pressrel/2002/pressrel_101602.pdf.

Printed and bound in Lebanon by International Press: interpress@int-press.com

Passport Contents

Unit 1 Getting Started

In this first unit, you will be looking at the following:
- Reasons for giving oral presentations
- The structure of oral presentations
- Opening an oral presentation
- Main themes and sub-themes in oral presentations
- Speaking effectively: Using pauses and varying your tone

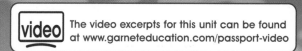

video — The video excerpts for this unit can be found at www.garneteducation.com/passport-video

1 Reasons for giving oral presentations

1.1 People are often asked to give oral presentations, not only in Higher Education but also in the workplace. Why do you think this is? Discuss your ideas with a partner or in small groups.

1.2 Are there any hidden benefits in learning to give oral presentations? Again, discuss your ideas with a partner or in small groups.

2 The structure of oral presentations

Unlike a spontaneous conversation, which can develop in any number of different directions depending on the speakers, an oral presentation tends to follow a fairly predictable structure with clearly marked stages. This is because in an oral presentation, it is very important that the listeners are able to follow – and later remember – what was said. Structuring an oral presentation in a logical and clear way really helps the listeners to do this.

2.1 Five typical stages of an academic oral presentation are listed in the shaded box below, but their order has been mixed up. Decide the order in which these different stages should occur and then write them in the spaces provided.

| The body | The chance for discussion | The overview | The general introduction | The conclusion |

STAGE 1: _____

STAGE 2: _____

STAGE 3: _____

STAGE 4: _____

STAGE 5: _____

2.2 Now match the following descriptions of what happens at each different stage. Write the correct letters in the second column in Exercise 2.1.

a) The speaker talks about the presentation topic in detail.
b) The speaker lets the audience know that he/she is going to finish the presentation.
c) The speaker greets the audience and introduces him/herself.
d) The speaker gives the audience the opportunity to ask questions.
e) The speaker tells the audience what the topic of the presentation will be.

3 Opening an oral presentation

3.1 🎧 1 You will now hear the openings of two quite different oral presentations. In each case, as you listen, make a note of:

a) what the speaker intends to talk about.
b) whether or not the audience already knows the speaker. How can you tell?

3.2 Look carefully at the example openings in the Language focus box below and discuss the following questions with a partner or in small groups:

- Which tenses can speakers use to let the audience know what they are intending to do?
- Which verbs can speakers use to show this intention? (e.g., *look at, describe* ...) Make a list of as many such verbs as you can think of.

Language focus 1   Opening phrases

In my presentation today, I'm going to look at some of the issues affecting tourism in Thailand.

In this presentation, I'll be describing the main forms of cancer that we are currently finding in women over the age of 40.

For the next ten minutes or so, I'd like to give you some of the reasons why most modern historians think the First World War started.

In my talk this morning, I'm going to focus on three of Monet's paintings.

In my presentation, I'll talk about four key effects that acid rain is having on our environment.

3.3 Match appropriate prepositions from the box below with the presentation verbs a–f. The first one has been done for you, but be careful – not every one of these verbs needs to be followed by a preposition.

> on   about   at

a) talk _about_

b) outline

c) describe

d) explain

e) look

f) focus

3.4 Work with a partner. Use language from Language focus 1 on page 5 to practise giving openings for the following presentation topics. Vary the language that you use each time and try to do the openings without looking at your book.

a) Inflation and the British economy
b) The life and times of Salvador Dali
c) Factors causing the spread of HIV
d) The impact of the Industrial Revolution on European society
e) Free topic (you choose)

Oral presentation top tip 1
Make plenty of eye contact

When people give an oral presentation for the first time, they often feel shy or embarrassed about standing up and speaking in public. To escape from their shyness and embarrassment, they may try to hide behind their notes or even talk to the projector screen rather than to the audience. Either way, the longer they avoid looking at the audience, the harder it becomes, and this can create a vicious cycle of nervousness; in some cases, almost an oral presentation phobia.

When you give an oral presentation, it is extremely important that you make *regular* eye contact with your audience right from the very beginning. By looking at people while you are speaking to them, you can make sure that you have their full attention. You can also make them feel that you are speaking to each one of them individually, a good technique for giving your talk greater impact. Finally, by looking people in the eye, you can judge their reactions to what you are saying. This can be particularly useful if the purpose of your presentation is to persuade them to do something.

Ways to feel more confident about making eye contact

- Rather than thinking 'All these people are looking at me. I feel so nervous!', try to turn the situation around by thinking, 'All these people are here just to listen to me. I feel so important!'

- Stand in an empty room. Practise looking to your far left, then shift your gaze to the middle, then look to the far right. Now look to the middle again and then shift your gaze back to the far left. Finally, look back to the middle. Slowly do this exercise a few times, making sure that you move your head each time, not just your eyes. When you feel comfortable about looking around you like this, vary the times that you let your gaze stay in any one place: for example, two seconds on the left, four seconds in the middle, two seconds on the right. When you find a speed that feels good for you, try doing the exercise while you say your name and introduce your presentation topic. When you can do this smoothly, ask three other students to join you. One should stand on your very far left, one should stand in the middle and the other should stand on your very far right. Practise giving your name and introducing your presentation topic while making eye contact with each student in turn: you must make eye contact with each student at least once.

4   Main themes and sub-themes in oral presentations

As discussed earlier in this unit, the second stage of an oral presentation can be called the *overview*. In this stage, the speaker usually says what the main topic or theme of the oral presentation will be and then divides this into suitable sub-themes.

Speakers do this because it makes it much easier for the audience to follow the presentation. It also means that the presentation develops a logical flow with clearly defined sections.

4.1   🎧2 You will now hear the general introduction and overview stages of two different oral presentations. In each case, listen carefully and make a note of the main theme and then the sub-themes.

Presentation 1:

Source: Jane Brown/Guardian News & Media Limited/2003

Presentation 2:

Main theme _____

Sub-themes _____

Main theme _____

Sub-themes _____

4.2 Look carefully at the example overviews in the Language focus box below and discuss the following questions with a partner or in small groups:

    a) What different phrases can speakers use to categorize and order the information that they want their presentation to cover?

    b) How can speakers link two or more points under one sub-theme?

Language focus 2 — Giving an overview

a) In my presentation today, I'm going to talk about images of violence in the movies of Quentin Tarantino. I'll start by looking at Pulp Fiction, arguably his best-known work. Next, I'll focus on Reservoir Dogs, and to finish off, I'll consider Kill Bill.

b) For the next 20 minutes or so, I'm going to look at some of the different factors that have an impact on international communication. Basically, I've divided my presentation into three parts. In the first part, I'll talk about cultural values and the way that these determine human behaviour. Then, in the second part, I'll look at the way that linguistic differences have an impact on how we think and the way in which we express ourselves. In the final part, I'll focus on non-verbal communication and consider the ways in which gestures, facial expressions and body posture can all transmit meaning just as effectively as words.

4.3 Use language from Language focus 2 on page 8 to complete the gaps in the passages below and fully develop presentation frameworks *a* and *b*. In framework *b*, the points that you will need to link under each sub-theme have been connected by an arrow.

a) Typical London tourist attractions:

Buckingham Palace

The British Museum

The Tower of London

In my presentation this morning, ... typical London

tourist attractions. .... Buckingham Palace,

.... the most popular attraction for tourists.

.... the British Museum,

.... the Tower of London.

b) Different effects of global warming:

melting glaciers ⟶	rising sea levels
climate change ⟶	wild animals' behaviour and habitat
retreating snowlines ⟶	death of certain species of trees

For the next 20 minutes or so, ...

different effects of global warming. Basically, ...

In the .... , I'll .... the melting glaciers and

.... are contributing to rising sea levels.

Then, ... give you

some examples of how this is having a serious impact on

.... and .... And in the

.... , ... and

consider how these are causing the ....

9

4.4 🎧 **3** Now listen to a recording of two speakers actually giving these presentation overviews. Check that you managed to fill in the gaps appropriately.

4.5 Work with a partner. Practise delivering the presentation frameworks about London tourist attractions and the different effects of global warming. Try to make your delivery sound like the speakers in the recordings.

5 Speaking effectively: Using pauses and varying your tone

Good speakers know how to vary the tone of their voice and when and where they should pause in order to create maximum impact. No matter how accurate your English may be *grammatically*, if you deliver an oral presentation in a monotone, without pausing in the right places, it will lack sufficient impact and not succeed in getting the audience's attention.

An inexperienced speaker can find silence quite worrying and will tend to avoid pausing. By making a deliberate effort to pause and look at the audience, you will find you can start taking control of the presentation rather than have the presentation taking control of you.

5.1 🎧 **4** Listen again to the recording of the presentation about global warming. As you listen, mark // on the transcript below to indicate all the places in which the speaker pauses. The first one has been done for you as an example.

For the next 20 minutes or so // I'm going to look at some of the different effects of global warming basically I've divided my presentation into three parts in the first part I'll talk about the melting glaciers and the way that these are contributing to rising sea levels then in the second part I'll look at climate change and give you some examples of how this is having a serious impact on wild animals' behaviour and habitat and in the final part I'll focus on the retreating snowlines and consider how these are causing the death of certain species of trees

5.2 Develop the oral presentation framework below and practise delivering it to the person sitting next to you. Make sure that you use the language covered in this unit and that you pause in all the appropriate places.

Ways to improve your English
- Reading English books and magazines
- Listening to radio and watching TV
- Socializing with English-speaking friends

---

6 Individual study

Develop an oral presentation framework around a topic related to your chosen field of study. Prepare to deliver this to your teacher and other students in your group in the next lesson.

End of Unit Checklist

You have now completed Unit 1. Read through the statements below and make a record of your progress by ticking the most appropriate boxes. As you complete the checklist, be prepared to think about what you can or can't do well. Use the activity to help you reflect on your progress.

5 = I feel very confident about this.

4 = I feel confident about this.

3 = I feel quite confident about this.

2 = I don't feel very confident about this.

1 = I still don't understand this at all.

For anything that you rate as a 2 or a 1, go back to that part of the unit and look at the material again.

	5	4	3	2	1
I know why oral presentations are often used in Higher Education and in the workplace.					
I can see some of the hidden benefits in learning to give oral presentations.					
I know how oral presentations are typically structured.					
I know how to introduce myself to people who already know me and people who don't know me.					
I know how to use a range of different verbs to introduce my main theme.					
I know two different ways of introducing my main theme and then my sub-themes.					
I know when and where to pause to help create impact.					

Unit 2 Organizing Your Material

In this unit, you will be looking at the following:

- Narrowing down the topic
- Leading in to a presentation
- Linking points in the presentation body
- Speaking effectively: Word stress
- Acknowledging academic sources
- Finishing an oral presentation

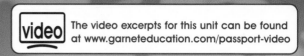

video   The video excerpts for this unit can be found at www.garneteducation.com/passport-video

1 Narrowing down the topic

As you learnt in Unit 1, when you give an oral presentation you should divide your main topic or theme into suitable sub-themes. Although there is no fixed rule for how many different sub-themes or parts that an oral presentation can have, a useful guide is to include no fewer than two, and no more than four.

1.1 Imagine you are going to give an oral presentation about the history of paper and want to use some of the information from the text on page 13. Read the text and identify four possible sub-themes. There is no right or wrong answer, and your choice will depend on the focus of your presentation.

1.2 Now write the titles for your sub-themes in the following framework:

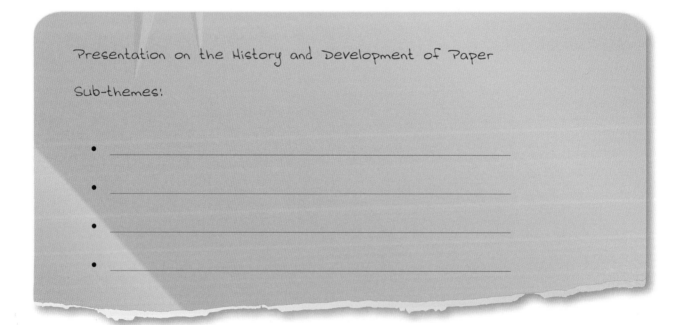

Presentation on the History and Development of Paper

Sub-themes:

- _____
- _____
- _____
- _____

1.3 Compare your ideas with another student. Are your presentation frameworks similar or different? Which one do you think is best? Why do you think this is?

The History and Development of Paper

Paper is a network of plant fibres laid down as a flat sheet. It is made from a suspension of plant tissues in water, known as pulp. Most pulp is made from wood, but recycled paper and other plant sources, including hemp, cotton and bamboo, can also be used.

The word *paper* is derived from the Egyptian 'papyrus', which was applied to sheets of writing material made by pressing together strips of the stems of the sedge, *Cyperus papyrus*. Paper as we now know it, made up of a mesh of randomly arranged plant fibres, was invented by the Chinese in the 2nd century AD.

In AD 105, a Chinese court official, Ts'ai Lun, produced a paper web from a slurry of paper mulberry (*Broussonetia papyrifera*) fibres in water. A small amount of the slurry was lifted up in a rectangular sieve consisting of a sheet of silk surrounded by a frame. The sieve was shaken gently to spread the fibres evenly and, as the water drained off, they settled to form a sheet, which was then dried in the sun. This process produced a long-lasting, high-quality paper, as can be seen from the samples preserved in the British Museum. Chinese paper makers found that they could vary the characteristics of the paper produced by using different plants as the sources of fibres.

Over 600 years later, a Chinese paper-making factory in Samarkand was captured by an Arab army. The Arab conquerors used the expertise of the Chinese paper makers to set up factories throughout the Muslim world, and paper-making techniques first arrived in Europe when the Moors conquered Spain. The raw materials for paper making were hemp and linen rags, including some from the wrappings of mummies. The first paper mill in Britain was built in Hertfordshire in 1488 and was referred to in a book printed by Caxton in 1490.

By 1800, paper-making factories were using 24 million tonnes of rags per year, and supplies of the raw material fell short of requirements. The search for a cheap, readily available and easily renewable substitute began. A French biologist observed that wasps' nests were made of a form of paper, which the wasps produced by macerating wood, and he suggested that wood might be a suitable material for paper makers to use. The first recorded use of wood for paper making in Europe was in 1769, but it was not until 1840 that paper made entirely from wood pulp appeared. The first newspaper to be made from an all-wood pulp, the *New York Times*, appeared in 1870.

The paper-making process was made faster and cheaper by the invention of the Fourdrinier paper-making machine, which used a continuous wire-mesh belt instead of individual paper moulds for forming a sheet of paper. This machine was first used in England in 1803 and finally ended the slow process of paper making by hand.

Paper is used for all types of printed material, from exercise books to encyclopedias. The type of paper varies according to the final use and lifetime of the product. Bank notes, which must be strong and durable, are made from high-quality pulp derived from new cotton rag trimmings and flax. Paper's absorbency is another valuable property that is put to good use in tissues and various other cloths used for soaking up liquids.

The packaging industry also depends on a continued supply of paper. It is combined with layers of plastic film, metallic foil or fabric in a process known as lamination. It is waterproofed, waxed or glazed, moulded or embossed, coloured, coated and printed. Recent developments in packaging of liquids use chemically produced pulp, bleached white and coated with plastic to form a clean, water-resistant, attractive container.

Other specialist products made from paper include insulation for electrical boards, printed circuits for the electronics industry, filters for many applications, disposable clothing for medical uses, bandages, car filters, fireworks and shotgun cartridges. Special treatments can be applied to make paper flame-resistant or capable of holding security information that is only visible under ultraviolet light. Paper can also be spun into string and used for tying and sealing or for making furniture and floor coverings.

The international character of paper is reflected by the fact that 90 countries produce paper and nearly every country in the world consumes it. In 1987, 212 million tonnes of paper were produced worldwide and 46 million tonnes entered world trade. In the UK, consumption per head of paper and paperboard in 1986 was about 143 kg, compared with 293 kg in the USA and less than 6 kg in India. However, the increased drive for literacy in developing countries will seriously affect the worldwide demand for writing and printing paper. A mere one per cent improvement in literacy in these countries could result in a significant increase in the annual consumption of paper-based products.

To meet the projected demand, foresters around the world have been breeding disease-resistant, fast-growing trees to increase the supply of pulpwood. For example, in 1984, 94 million genetically improved conifer seedlings of loblolly pine (*Pinus taeda*) were planted in US forests. Plantation owners there forecast that these trees, when mature, will meet the anticipated demand for pulp and paper in the USA well into the middle of the 21st century.

2   Leading in to a presentation

2.1   🎧**5** The transcript below shows the opening of an oral presentation about some famous British inventions. What do you think the speaker says next? Write your ideas in the space provided, then listen to the recording.

> In my presentation this morning, I'm going to talk about some famous British inventors and the products that they have developed. Basically, I've divided this presentation into three parts. In the first part, I'll talk about Alexander Graham Bell and the invention of the telephone. Then, in the second part, I'll look at the work of John Logie Baird and his development of the television. And to finish off, I'll discuss Alexander Fleming and his research on the antibiotic we now know as penicillin.

2.2   Look carefully at the example lead-in phrases listed in the Language focus box below and discuss the following questions with a partner or in small groups:

a) What do all of these phrases have in common?
b) What do they signal to the audience?

Language focus 3   Lead-in phrases

So, for starters then, let's look at ...

Right, to begin with, let's look at ...

Ok, let's start by looking at ...

2.3   Look back at the presentation framework that you prepared about the history and development of paper. Add a suitable lead-in phrase and take turns delivering your framework to a partner. Make sure that you pause in all the right places.

Oral presentation top tip 2
Pay attention to posture

When people are asked to give an oral presentation, they often feel very awkward about how they should stand and what they should do with their hands. Some people try to control their nerves by walking around and making exaggerated gestures. Unfortunately, mannerisms like this only tend to distract the audience and make the presenter seem even more nervous than he/she already is.

Other presenters go for what they think is the cool and casual approach and lean back while they're speaking with their hands in their pockets. However, this style of presenting can make it seem as if the speaker doesn't really care about the presentation and can come across as very arrogant and condescending.

When you give an oral presentation, you need to adopt a body posture that feels right for you. There are no absolute rules for this, but your posture should:
- be both comfortable and authoritative.
- allow you to be seen by everyone (stand up straight and keep your head high).
- be firm (don't sway from side to side).

It is helpful to use hand gestures in support of your speaking, but you should always try to keep your gestures fairly clear and concise rather than just waving your hands around uncontrollably. Always be aware of exactly *which* gestures you are using and *why*. You should also bear in mind that the meaning of hand gestures can differ widely across cultures.

Ways to improve your presentation posture and body language

- Stand in front of a full-length mirror. Try different ways of standing and holding your hands until you find a way that both feels comfortable and looks good.
- Still standing in front of the mirror, practise giving a presentation opening. While you are speaking, pay attention to what you are doing with your hands and body.
- Practise giving a presentation to your friends. Ask them for feedback on your posture and use of body language.
- Practise giving the presentation in the actual place where you will give the final presentation, if you can, using the same equipment you will be using on the day.

If possible, ask your teacher to record your presentation on video. When you watch the video, pay special attention to the way you are standing and what you are doing with your hands.

3   Linking points in the presentation body

3.1 🎧 **6** You are going to hear a presentation based on the framework below. Listen carefully and try to make a note of the phrases (a, b and c) that the speaker uses to link her sub-themes in the presentation body.

Theme: The IELTS examination

Lead-in phrases	Sub-themes
I will start by looking at ...	History and background ↓ Examination format ↓
a) _____	
	Scores and what they mean ↓
b) _____	
	Problems with IELTS ↓
c) _____	

3.2 Look carefully at the example linking phrases in the Language focus box below and discuss the following questions with a partner or in small groups:

- What are some common features of linking phrases, e.g., their position in the sentence?
- Can you think of any other verbs that you might use, e.g., *go on to*?

Language focus 4 — Linking phrases

Now I'd like to move on to the next part of my presentation, which is how Hitler got the support of the German people.

Next, I'd like to look at my second point today: some of the ways in which mobile phone technology has developed.

This leads us to my next point: suggestions for improving your English speaking.

This brings us to the final part of my presentation today: what countries can do to reduce their greenhouse gas emissions.

4 Speaking effectively: Word stress

Good speakers know which words they should stress in order to get their audience's attention and gain maximum impact. In the same way that knowing when to pause is an important part of effective speaking, knowing where to apply word stress can make all the difference between a presentation that is easy to follow and a presentation in which the audience is struggling to understand what the speaker is talking about.

4.1 🎧 7 Listen to some people using the lead-in phrases and linking phrases below. Underline the words on which the speaker puts the most stress. The first one has been done for you as an example.

a) <u>OK</u>, let's <u>start</u> by looking at where paper was actually <u>invented</u>.
b) So, for starters, let's look at the history of the telephone.
c) Now I'd like to move on to the next part of my presentation, which is how Hitler got the support of the German people.
d) Next, I'd like to look at my second point today: some of the ways in which mobile phone technology has developed.
e) This leads us to my next point: suggestions for improving your English speaking.
f) Right, I'm going to finish off today by looking at Alexander Fleming and the antibiotic penicillin.
g) This brings us to the final part of my presentation today: what countries can do to reduce their greenhouse gas emissions.

4.2 Look at the oral presentation framework below. Write two sentences (in note form if you prefer), adding your own content to each of the sub-themes.

Famous Blockbuster Movies

Titanic _____

_____

Gladiator _____

_____

Braveheart _____

_____

4.3 Practise delivering the presentation body to a partner. Start from the lead-in stage, e.g., *So let's start by looking at* Titanic … and make sure that you use appropriate linking phrases when you change from one sub-theme to another.

5   Acknowledging academic sources

In an academic oral presentation, as with most other types of academic assignment, it is important that you acknowledge any sources that you have used, in order to avoid being accused of plagiarism.

Some useful phrases for doing this *orally* are listed in the Language focus box below. We will look at how to reference academic sources in writing (on presentation slides) in Unit 5.

Language focus 5   Acknowledging sources

As a number of authors have pointed out, for example Seinfeld (1980), Barker (1987), Allen (1993) and most recently Watson (2011), Hitler badly underestimated the severity of the Russian winter, and this must be seen as a major factor in his failure to capture Moscow.

Writing in 2005, Johnson has put forward the view that governments should spend more money on primary, as opposed to secondary, education.

It seems that the literature on this subject can basically be divided into two camps. Some authors, for example Barnes (2003), Hamilton (2006) and Mackenzie (2009), suggest that global warming is a 100% man-made phenomenon. Other writers, for example Parker (2008), Fleming (2010) and Steed (2012), reject this view and contend that global warming is a natural occurrence and would happen anyway.

According to Fisher, in an article that he wrote in 2011, Kennedy's assassination was actually an elaborate plot masterminded by the CIA.

As Wallace, writing in 2007, has pointed out, even though we are becoming better at predicting natural disasters like earthquakes and tsunamis, the fact remains that we're powerless to prevent them.

5.1   Imagine that you are giving a presentation on environmental issues and the recycling of natural resources. As part of your background research, you have consulted academic sources A–D below.

Work with a partner and take turns making points and orally acknowledging the relevant sources, using appropriate phrases from the Language focus box opposite. An example has been done to help you.

Example

Writing in 2003, Potter has put forward the view that supermarkets should be legally required to replace plastic carrier bags with re-usable bags made of recycled paper.

SOURCE A

Potter, T. (2003). Working towards a greener future. *Journal of Sustainable Development, 22,* 14–22.

In terms of sheer waste of resources, supermarket chains in the UK are probably one of the biggest culprits. Literally millions and millions of plastic bags are thrown away every single day. However, if it was made a legal requirement that supermarkets should replace these plastic carrier bags with re-usable bags made of recycled paper, such unnecessary waste could be dramatically cut.

SOURCE B

Clark, B. (2006). *Green Ideals & corporate greed.* Cambridge: Cambridge University Press.

Take the ubiquitous plastic bag. These have become such a common sight in our supermarkets that most of us no longer question them. But just pause for a moment to consider the sheer waste, not to mention the environmental damage, that this seemingly innocuous item causes every single day.

SOURCE C

Cooper, R. (2009). If it's good for the planet, it's good for the company. *Journal of Corporate Ethics, 42,* 14–22.

After increasing pressure from environmental activists, two leading supermarket chains agreed to place an outright ban on the provision of disposable plastic bags, replacing them with re-usable bags made of recycled paper instead. As a further incentive for shoppers to 'think green', these same chains also introduced in-store collection points where surplus plastic bags could be traded in for redeemable shopping points.

SOURCE D

Tanner, S. (2010). Profit yes, but at what price? *The Environmentalist, 53,* 30–41.

However, it must be said that a recent initiative by one major supermarket to stop providing its shoppers with plastic bags has not been entirely well-received. In this particular case, a large number of customers staged a protest, threatening to boycott the store and take their trade elsewhere.

6 Finishing an oral presentation

When you reach the end of an oral presentation, you should let the audience know that you are going to finish by using a suitable ending phrase. It is not acceptable just to stop talking!

6.1 Look carefully at the example phrases for ending a presentation in the Language focus box below and discuss the following questions with a partner or in small groups:

- What are some common features of ending phrases?
- What single feature do *all* of these ending phrases have in common?
- What are three different ways that you can end an oral presentation?

Language focus 6 — Ending phrases

That concludes my presentation. Are there any questions?

That brings us to the end of my presentation today. Thank you very much for listening. Does anyone have any questions?

Right then, as I hope to have shown this morning, it's clear that Scotland has many attractions for foreign tourists. Now, does anyone have any questions?

I hope you've enjoyed my presentation today. If anyone has any questions, I'll do my best to answer them.

6.2 Choose **one** of the presentation frameworks below. Add one or two sentences of content for each sub-theme.

Music

- Classical _____

    _____

- Folk _____

    _____

- Rock _____

    _____

- Jazz _____

    _____

Free topic (you choose)

- _____
  _____
- _____
  _____
- _____
  _____
- _____
  _____

6.3   Deliver your framework as a mini presentation. Start by introducing yourself and end by asking if there are any questions. Don't forget to use key phrases from this unit to lead in, link each of the sub-themes in the presentation body and let the audience know when you are ending.

7   Individual study

Look back at the subject-specific oral presentation framework that you prepared at the end of Unit 1. Add a few sentences of content to each of the sub-themes to flesh this presentation out and prepare to deliver it to your teacher and classmates as a full presentation in the next class. You should aim to talk for at least three minutes.

End of Unit Checklist

You have now completed Unit 2. Read through the statements below and make a record of your progress by ticking the most appropriate boxes.

5 = I feel very confident about this.

4 = I feel confident about this.

3 = I feel quite confident about this.

2 = I don't feel very confident about this.

1 = I still don't understand this at all.

For anything that you rate as a 2 or a 1, go back to that part of the unit and look at the material again.

	5	4	3	2	1
I know how to narrow down a presentation topic and divide it into suitable sub-themes.					
I know how to use some different phrases for leading into a presentation.					
I know how to use some different phrases for linking the sub-themes in a presentation body.					
I know how to change my voice stress to gain the maximum clarity and impact.					
I know how my posture and body language can have an impact on a presentation.					
I know how to acknowledge academic sources.					
I know how to use some different techniques and phrases for ending an oral presentation.					

Unit 3 Dealing with Q&A

In this unit, you will be looking at the following:

- Asking questions after oral presentations
- Types of questions after oral presentations
- Speaking effectively: Intonation
- Answering questions after oral presentations
- Closing an oral presentation

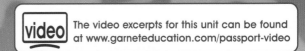
The video excerpts for this unit can be found at www.garneteducation.com/passport-video

1 Asking questions after oral presentations

As you learnt in Unit 2, at the end of an oral presentation it is polite for the presenter to ask the audience if they have any questions. This gives people the chance to clarify anything that they weren't sure about or to ask the presenter for extra information.

1.1 You are going to hear a presentation about the Loch Ness monster, a legendary creature that some people believe exists in Scotland. First, match the words on the left with the definitions on the right. An example has been done for you.

Words	Definitions
paranormal	go beneath the surface
sturgeon	an attempt to make people believe something that isn't true
cryptozoology	a piece of wood, typically in a cylindrical shape
statistician	the study of animals that don't exist, according to science
hump	someone who studies data and statistics
binoculars	a type of aquatic dinosaur
authenticity	a long thin fish that looks like a snake
hoax	the supernatural; something that cannot be explained by science
plesiosaur	an optical instrument that can be used to make faraway objects seem closer
submerge	a large round shape that rises above the surface
computer enhancement	something that kills and eats other animals
eel	the quality of being real, true or genuine
log	a type of large freshwater fish
predator	a technical process used to improve the quality of photographs and films

1.2 🎧 **8** Now listen to the presentation and try to think of some questions that you might like to ask the presenter. The names of some people that he mentions have been given to help you:

- Mr and Mrs Mackay
- The London Surgeon
- Tim Dinsdale

Make a note of your questions in the space below.

_____

_____

_____

_____

_____

_____

2 Types of questions after oral presentations

There are three main types of questions that people tend to ask after oral presentations. These are shown in the box below.

Type	Style of question
1	The 'Straight' question
2	The 'Give me more' question
3	The 'I didn't understand, so tell me again' question

2.1 Read through questions a–l. Decide which type of question each one is an example of and write 1, 2 or 3 next to it. The first one has been done for you.

a) In your presentation, you said that there were other sightings of the monster on land apart from the Spicers'. Can you say a little more about those sightings? **2**

b) I have a question. Do you think the monster might just be a very large otter?

c) I wasn't sure what you meant when you said that the Spicers saw the monster carrying something in its mouth. Can you go over that part again?

d) You said that the surgeon's photograph may actually have been a hoax. Can you go into a bit more detail on how exactly the hoax might have been carried out?

e) You mentioned that Loch Morar on the west coast is actually deeper than Loch Ness. Haven't similar animals been sighted there, too?

f) I still don't understand why the monster can't be a plesiosaur. Can you explain that part again?

g) If there is a Loch Ness monster or family of monsters, why don't we find any remains of them around the loch? I mean, if these animals have been in the loch since the 6th century, then there must be some bones or something in there …

h) I'd like to ask something. When was the most recent sighting of the monster?

i) In your presentation, you said that you think a sturgeon is the most likely candidate for the monster. I can see how this might account for sightings of humps and water disturbances, but how would it explain sightings of the head and neck?

j) You said that Tim Dinsdale's film was computer-enhanced. Can you say a bit more about the procedures that are actually involved in that?

k) You didn't actually say anything about the search for Nessie underwater. What work has been done at Loch Ness using sonar?

l) What are the different types of fish in Loch Ness?

2.2 Some examples of language used in the three main question types are detailed in the Language focus box below. What particular language is used to refer back to something that the presenter said? Can you think of any other phrases for doing this?

Language focus 7 — Question types

1 'Straight' questions
a Why is the monster unlikely to be a plesiosaur?
b I have a question. Why is the monster unlikely to be a plesiosaur?
c You mentioned that the monster is unlikely to be a plesiosaur. Why do you think that is?

2 'Give me more' questions
In your presentation, you said that the sturgeon theory can't account for every single sighting:
a Can you go into more detail about that?
b Can you say a little more about that?
c Can you give us some examples of that?

3 'I didn't understand, so tell me again' questions
I'm not very clear on how the process of computer enhancement works:
a Can you explain about that again?
b Can you go over that part again?
c Can you run through that again?

2.3 Look back at the questions that you prepared for Exercise 1.2. Where necessary, use phrases from the Language focus box to improve your questions, and then practise asking them aloud.

3 Speaking effectively: Intonation

Intonation refers to the way that our voice falls or rises when we speak. Good presenters are very much aware of intonation because they know that it can affect the meaning of what is said.

A speaker's intonation indicates several things. Firstly, it tells us whether he or she is stating a fact or raising a question. It also tells us when the speaker is coming to the end of a sentence or section of the presentation, and when he or she is going to start a new point. Intonation also gives us clues about the emotional state of the speaker. A sharp rise or fall indicates strong emotion, e.g., surprise or excitement, whereas flat intonation signals emotional distance or even boredom.

3.1   🎧9 Listen to the two recordings of the statement below. In each case, does the speaker's intonation rise or fall? What effect does the intonation pattern have on the meaning? Complete the chart.

• The surgeon's photograph was a hoax.

Recording	Rising or falling?	Effect on meaning?
1		
2		

3.2   🎧10 Listen to the recording of sentences *a–e*. Mark whether or not the speakers' intonation rises ↑ or falls ↓ on the words that are underlined.

a) Three quite common causes of monster sightings at Loch Ness are <u>boat wakes</u>, <u>mirage effects</u> and <u>floating tree trunks</u>.

b) Sonar readings have proved that the monster exists, <u>haven't they</u>?

c) Sonar readings can sometimes be false, <u>can't they</u>?

d) Why not use a <u>submarine</u>?

e) That brings us to the end of my <u>presentation</u>.

3.3   Sentences *a–e* are all examples of some common intonation patterns in English. What do you think these are? Discuss your ideas with a partner.

3.4   🎧11 Now listen to the recording of another two statements. What do you notice about the intonation of the words that are underlined?

- The monster <u>may</u> just be a large fish.
- It's <u>possible</u> that the witnesses were simply mistaken.

3.5   Work with a partner. Take turns reading sentences *a–g* aloud, paying particular attention to your intonation for the words that have been underlined.

   a) The works of three authors have been particularly influential at Loch Ness: <u>Rupert Gould</u>, <u>Constance Whyte</u> and <u>Tim Dinsdale</u>.

   b) The surgeon's photograph was exposed as a hoax in 1994, <u>wasn't it</u>?

   c) Newspaper reports aren't always very reliable though, <u>are they</u>?

   d) It <u>may</u> be that the monster feeds off the mud and sediment at the bottom of the loch.

   e) Could the loch be <u>drained</u>?

   f) It's <u>possible</u> that head and neck sightings are simply tree branches floating in the water.

   g) Scientists last visited the loch in <u>2003</u>.

3.6   🎧12 Now listen to the recording of sentences *a–g*. Was your intonation the same?

4   Answering questions after oral presentations

In the same way that there are a number of phrases for asking questions, we can also identify language that is useful for giving answers.

4.1   🎧13 Listen to how the presenter deals with questions after his presentation about the Loch Ness monster. Make a note of the phrases he uses to acknowledge each question in the table on page 28 before he gives an answer.

Question	Response
a) I have a question. Do you think the monster might be a large otter?	It's certainly true that otters may have accounted for some of the sightings, particularly the ones on land.
b) I still don't understand why the monster can't be a plesiosaur. Can you explain that part again?	Let me try again. The main difficulty with the plesiosaur theory is that it's hard to see how such a creature could have got into the loch in the first place.
c) So what do you mean when you said that unexplained sightings are simply cases of mistaken identity?	There are a number of factors at Loch Ness that make it particularly easy for people to get confused.

4.2 🎧 **14** Listen to the presenter giving more information in response to the questions. Make a note of the evidence he gives for each question.

a) the monster being a large otter

_____

_____

b) why the monster can't be a plesiosaur

_____

_____

c) things that can cause people to see monsters

_____

_____

4.3 Sometimes you may simply not know the answer to the audience's questions. In cases like this, rather than pretending, or attempting to bluff your way out, it's usually best just to admit your lack of knowledge. You can always offer to find out the answer for someone later.

Some useful phrases for doing this are listed in the Language focus box at the top of the next page.

When you simply don't know ...

Sorry, I'm afraid I don't know the answer to that.

Sorry, I'm afraid you've got me there; I simply don't know. I can try to find out for you though. See me after the presentation and we can sort something out.

Sorry, I have to be honest with you and say that I don't know.

4.4 Work with a partner. You are going to practise asking and answering questions. One of you is Person A and the other one is Person B. Look at page 31 and follow the instructions. Person A should begin by saying, 'That brings us to the end of my presentation. Does anyone have any questions?' Swap roles after finishing the task and do it again.

5 Closing an oral presentation

After dealing with questions from the audience, presenters should formally close their presentation. Some useful phrases for doing this are listed in the Language focus box below.

5.1 🎧 **15** Listen to the recording and then practise saying these phrases out loud.

Language focus 9

Closing phrases

a Does anyone have any more questions? (no questions)
In that case, I'll finish my presentation here. Thank you for listening.

b If there are no more questions, I'll stop here. Thank you very much for your attention.

6 Individual study

Look back at the oral presentation you prepared at the end of Unit 2. If *you* had been listening to this presentation, what questions might you have asked? Using key phrases from this unit, write down at least three questions and practise both asking and answering them yourself out loud. If possible, try to record your voice while doing this.

Oral presentation top tip 3
Controlling your nerves

For many students, giving an oral presentation can be a nerve-wracking experience and something that they dread having to do. For shy students, in particular, standing up in public and speaking in a foreign language may seem like a major ordeal. Unfortunately, as you learnt in Unit 1, oral presentations are becoming an increasingly important feature of university life.

However, all is not lost. The good news is that a basic understanding of how the human body reacts to stress, along with some practice in using stress management techniques, can really help to make the whole situation much more bearable.

Stress and the human body

Whenever we feel stress, the body starts to release the hormone *adrenaline* into the bloodstream. Adrenaline increases the heartbeat, raises the blood pressure and can cause other bodily reactions such as sweating or shaking. Basically, adrenaline is our body's way of giving us some extra energy to deal with life's difficult situations, occasions that are often referred to in textbooks as 'fight or flight'. Even if you're not aware of feeling nervous *mentally* before giving an oral presentation, physically your body will still be preparing itself.

Of course, a certain amount of nervous energy can be a good thing because it keeps you alert. Oral presentations *ought* to be challenging, so you shouldn't expect to get rid of your nervousness completely. However, the secret of being a successful speaker is in knowing how to control that nervousness and making your nervous energy work *for* you rather than against you.

A simple way to relax is to put the presentation right out of your mind before you begin. This is best done up to half an hour before you begin, once you are thoroughly prepared. You will find that trying hard to remember what to do right up to the start of the presentation is actually counterproductive.

A routine to help you relax

Most books about stress management mention the importance of effective breathing, especially deep exhalation, or letting all your breath out. This is central to the relaxation technique below, adapted from Sandy Linver's book, *Speak and Get Results* (1994, Fireside, New York).

a) First go through some basic stretching exercises to help you get rid of tension in your back and neck muscles: push your shoulders back; bend your spine; gently move your head up and down and from side to side.

b) Sit down, close your eyes and make a conscious decision to let yourself go. Keep your head upright, but let all your muscles relax. Feel yourself sinking deeply into your seat.

c) Breathe out deeply. When you think you've finished exhaling, try to let out a little more. You should be able to feel your ribcage dropping every time that you breathe out. Practise exhaling in this way a number of times.

d) Scan your body for areas of tension. When you find a place that still feels tense, mentally focus on getting your muscles to relax at that point. Keep doing this until you can find no more tension points.

If you practise this routine regularly, it will become an effective stress reliever that you can apply whenever you have to do something that makes you nervous.

Prompts for Exercise 4.4

Person A: Read the instructions below.
Person B: Turn the page upside down and read your instructions.

Instructions for Person A

You have just given a presentation about the Loch Ness monster. If anyone has any questions, you must do your best to answer them. In each case, make sure that you preface your answer with appropriate language to suit the question type.

Begin by saying, 'That brings us to the end of my presentation. Does anyone have any questions?'

Key information to help you answer any questions

- Sonar is like an underwater version of radar. It works by sending electronic sound impulses into the water. When these impulses hit an object, they reflect back and cause an echo that can be shown on a computer screen.

- The monster couldn't be a whale because, just like sharks, whales are saltwater animals. Loch Ness is a freshwater lake.

- Loch Morar has a similar monster tradition to Loch Ness, and there have been a number of expeditions there over the years. The Loch Morar monster is known as Morag, and Loch Morar is the deepest lake in the British Isles.

- As well as the monster, there have also been a number of UFO sightings reported from Loch Ness. Some people believe that monsters and UFOs are somehow connected.

- We shouldn't expect every sonar contact in Loch Ness to represent the monster. Some sonar echoes may in fact just be mistakes caused by the sonar beam bouncing back from rocks under the water.

- The surgeon's photograph from 1934 was exposed as a fake 60 years later – apparently, the picture shows a model mounted on a toy submarine. Another famous photograph from the 1950s also turned out to be a fake – in that case, the photo was of bales of hay covered with black plastic bags.

Instructions for Person B

Ask your partner the following questions. In each case, you should preface your question with appropriate language to suit the question type.

'Straight' questions

- You want to know how sonar works.
- You want to know if the monster could be a whale.

'Give me more' questions

- The presenter said that Loch Morar also has a monster tradition. You want to know more about that.
- The presenter said that other mysteries have been reported from Loch Ness, apart from the monster. You want to know more about that.

'I didn't understand, so tell me again' questions

- The presenter said that not every sonar contact in Loch Ness is likely to be accurate. Ask him/her to explain that again.
- The presenter said that some of the most famous photographs are now known to be fakes. Ask him/her to explain that again.

End of Unit Checklist

You have now completed Unit 3. Read through the statements below and make a record of your progress by ticking the most appropriate boxes.

5 = I feel very confident about this.

4 = I feel confident about this.

3 = I feel quite confident about this.

2 = I don't feel very confident about this.

1 = I still don't understand this at all.

For anything that you rate as a 2 or a 1, go back to that part of the unit and look at the material again.

	5	4	3	2	1
I know some useful phrases for asking questions at the end of an oral presentation.					
I know some different effects that intonation can have on the meaning of spoken English.					
I know how to modify my own intonation to achieve these effects.					
I know some useful phrases for dealing with questions at the end of an oral presentation.					
I know how to close an oral presentation.					
I know how stress and nerves are likely to affect my body.					
I know how to apply some techniques for controlling my nerves before giving an oral presentation.					

Unit 4 Creating More Impact

In this unit, you will be looking at the following:
- Alternative ways to open an oral presentation
- The language of alternative openings
- Speaking effectively: Word stress and meaning
- Language for increasing the impact of presentations
- Rhetorical questions, repetition and the rule of threes
- Achieving maximum impact when presenting numbers and data

> **video** The video excerpts for this unit can be found at www.garneteducation.com/passport-video

1 Alternative ways to open an oral presentation

Speakers often choose a different style of presentation opening to help them get the audience's attention. However, deciding to use an alternative opening is not without its risks: if things go wrong, it may ruin the whole presentation.

1.1 🎧 **16** You are going to hear four different openings for the same presentation. As you listen, make notes under headings *a*, *b* and *c*.

a) How do each of the openings differ?

_____

_____

b) Which opening do you think was best? Why?

_____

_____

c) Which opening do you think was least effective? Why?

_____

_____

1.2 Common alternative opening techniques are listed on the next page. Discuss these questions with a partner:

- Which technique(s) would you use?
- Do you think that certain techniques are better suited to some topics than others?
- Are there any that you would not use?

a) The presenter tells the audience some shocking or surprising facts.

b) The presenter asks the audience a question.

c) The presenter tells the audience a joke or a funny story.

d) The presenter asks the audience to do something.

e) The presenter shows the audience a picture, slide or photograph, or asks them to listen to something.

1.3 Which of the above techniques *wasn't* used in the different presentation openings for Exercise 1.1? Why do you think this is?

2   The language of alternative openings

🎧 **17** Some examples of language used for alternative openings are given in the Language focus box below. Listen to the recording and then practise saying these phrases out loud.

Language focus 10   Alternative openings

Asking the audience a question
a Before I start my presentation today, I'd like to ask you all a question. [QUESTION] Put your hand up, please, if your answer is yes.

b Good afternoon, everyone. Before we get started, I have a quick question. [QUESTION] Please raise your hand if the answer is yes.

Asking the audience to do something
a Before I start my presentation today, I'd like to carry out a little experiment. Can you stand up, please, if you've had any junk food in the last week?

b Good morning, everyone. Before we get started, I have a little task for you. Can you stand up, please, if you've had any junk food in the last week?

Getting the audience's attention with some unexpected information
Good afternoon, everyone. Before I start my presentation today, I'd like to share a few facts with you. As you probably all know, Scotland has the highest mountain in the whole of the UK. You may also have heard that Scotland has the largest freshwater lake in the UK. But I wonder how many of you realize that, according to a recent survey, Scotland has the highest incidence of teenage obesity, not only in the UK, but in all of Europe?

2.1   Choose one of the oral presentation topics below and prepare an alternative opening using appropriate language and techniques from Language focus 10 on page 34.

Global Warming and Climate Change

Alcohol Abuse

Poverty and Famine in the Developing World

The International AIDS Crisis

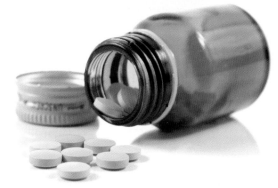

3   Speaking effectively: Word stress and meaning

🎧 **18** As we discussed in Unit 2, effective speakers know how to use word stress to create more impact. Stressing words that would normally be unstressed or contracted is a common way of doing this. Look at the examples below and listen to the recording.

a) The situation isn't going to improve. ⟶ The situation is **NOT** going to improve.

b) There wasn't any point in them doing that. ⟶ There was **NO** point in them doing that.

c) It's been a very difficult time. ⟶ It **HAS** been a very difficult time.

3.1   🎧 **19** Rewrite statements *a–f*, giving them greater impact by changing the word stress. Practise saying the new versions out loud, then compare yourself with the recording.

a) Global warming isn't going to go away by itself.

b) We're trying to do something about it.

c) It's been difficult to convince people.

d) It's a worldwide issue.

e) We can't ignore what the planet is telling us.

f) We're going to have to change our habits.

4 Language for increasing the impact of presentations

In addition to the techniques already mentioned, speakers can increase the impact of their presentations by applying special linguistic devices such as *rhetorical questions, adverbs of degree* and *strategic repetition.*

4.1   Look at the extract below and underline the rhetorical question.

This city is famous for many things. We have a beautiful castle; we have one of the best universities in the country and we have a fantastic theatre for the live arts. But do you know what else we have? One of the highest incidences of drug and alcohol abuse …

4.2   Rewrite statements *b* and *c* below, filling the gaps by using a similar rhetorical question. An example has been done to help you.

Example

a) These days, we hear about climate change and global warming in almost every single news broadcast, so it's easy to become complacent about it; to think that the issue is somebody else's problem and not ours. One hundred people were interviewed recently on Channel 4. *What do you think they said?* They said that in their opinion, nothing they could do would make any difference.

b) British children are eating more junk food than ever before. _____
    _____ Well, one effect is that teenage obesity is becoming a major problem.

c) The WHO has reported that around six million children under the age of five die from malnutrition every year. _____
    Well, it basically means 11 deaths every minute.

4.3   🎧 **20** Rewrite statements *b–d* below, giving them greater impact by adding an adverb of degree (*highly, extremely, hardly,* etc.). An example has been done to help you. Practise saying the new versions out loud, then compare yourself with the recording.

Example

a) It is unlikely to change. ⟶ It is **HIGHLY** unlikely to change.

b) The long-term effects of global warming are worrying.

    _____

c) Doctors are becoming concerned about teenage obesity.

    _____

d) If the WHO receives more funding, the number of deaths can be reduced.

    _____

4.4   🎧 **21** Speakers often use repetition as a deliberate means of adding extra emphasis to what they say. Listen to the recording of three excerpts from a presentation about global warming. Make a note of which words the speaker repeats. What do all of these words have in common?

4.5   🎧 **22** Rewrite statements *a–d* below using the repetition technique to create more impact. Practise saying your rewritten statements out loud and then compare yourself with the recording.

   a) Without doubt, the current situation is very serious.

   _____

   b) If we received more funding, we could save many lives.

   _____

   c) Our distribution networks are much better than they used to be.

   _____

   d) It is far easier to prevent a problem from happening than to solve it later.

   _____

4.6   🎧 **23** Listen to three more excerpts from the presentation about global warming. Which words does the speaker repeat this time? What do all of these words have in common?

4.7   🎧 **24** Rewrite statements *a–d* below using the doubling technique to create more impact. Practise saying your rewritten statements out loud and then compare yourself with the recording.

   a) The temperature of the sea is getting warmer.

   _____

   b) More people are becoming concerned.

   _____

   c) Public opinion is growing stronger.

   _____

   d) The weather is becoming less predictable.

   _____

5 Rhetorical questions, repetition and the rule of threes

For maximum impact, speakers may choose to combine a number of different techniques. We have already considered rhetorical questions and the use of repetition; speakers may also decide to use a technique called the 'rule of threes'.

As its name suggests, the rule of threes refers to when speakers choose their three most important points and mention them in order.

5.1 Look at the example below, in which a speaker is talking about the prevention of teenage drug abuse. Underline each of the techniques that are being used and label them – the first one has been done for you.

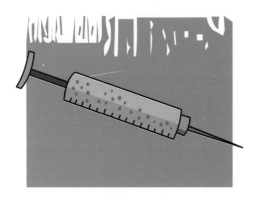  

Example

So what do we need to do? **(rhetorical question)** The answers are very clear.

- We need to educate teenagers better about the harmful effects of drugs.
- We need to keep a closer watch on the pubs and clubs where drugs are available.
- And we need to introduce much harsher penalties for the drug dealers.

5.2 Choose <u>one</u> of the presentation scenarios below and use a rhetorical question, repetition and the rule of threes to make a statement with maximum impact.

a) You are giving a presentation about ways to reduce litter around the city.
b) You are giving a presentation about ways that your institution could make things better for international students.
c) You are giving a presentation about improving the standard of living in your home country.
d) Free topic (you choose).

Oral presentation top tip 4
Voice projection
Using your voice effectively

A common problem when people are asked to give an oral presentation is that they fail to project their voice. No matter how good your English is or how interesting the content of your presentation might be, if the audience can't hear what you are saying, then the presentation will not be a success. It is absolutely essential that you learn to use your voice as effectively as possible. However, voice projection does not mean shouting: it simply means making your voice carry as far as possible with the minimum of effort.

How your voice works

Effective voice projection has a lot to do with effective breathing. As you may have noticed, our voice is produced when we breathe out. Each time that we exhale, the muscles in our abdomen force air out of our lungs and through the voice box, or larynx, which is located in our throat. The vocal cords inside the larynx vibrate when air passes through them, and this is what makes sound. Before you speak, therefore, it is important that you breathe in properly, because it is the inhaled breath that provides the energy for your voice.

The practice exercise below is designed to make you more aware of your breathing and help you achieve better voice projection.

A voice projection practice breathing activity

1   Stand in front of a long mirror (you need to be able to see yourself down to the waist).
2   Take in a deep breath and watch what happens to your shoulders. If they rise up as you breathe in, it probably means that you're breathing with the upper part of your lungs. The objective is for you to breathe from much lower down.
3   Breathe in deeply again, but this time, try to keep your shoulders down and focus on feeling your lower ribcage expand. If you can feel your lower ribcage expanding as you breathe in, it means that the air is getting into the right place.
4   Breathe out and concentrate on actually pushing all the air out, instead of just letting it flow out by itself. The muscle that you are using to push all the air out is your diaphragm. For good voice projection, you will need to be able to use your diaphragm effectively.
5   Practise breathing in and breathing out until you can really feel your diaphragm working and know how to push with it when you exhale.
6   Take in a deep breath, but this time when you breathe out, say 'Aaaah'. Push with your diaphragm and focus on feeling the air rise up through your body, into your throat and out of your mouth. You should notice that the harder you push with your diaphragm, the louder your 'Aaaah' noise can become.

Practise saying individual words in this way and then build up to short sentences. By learning to control your diaphragm like this, you will be able to project your voice better and be a more effective public speaker.

6 Achieving maximum impact when presenting numbers and data

6.1 🎧 **25** You are going to hear three pairs of sentences. For each pair, tick the sentence that you think has the most impact. Be prepared to explain why you think that is.

First pair	Second pair	Third pair
Sentence A:	Sentence A:	Sentence A:
Sentence B:	Sentence B:	Sentence B:

6.2 Choose one of the facts below and present it to your classmates so that they can easily relate to the data and you gain maximum impact.

a) In the Battle of the Somme during the First World War, about 60,000 British soldiers were killed in the first hour.

b) There are about 45 miles of nerves in the human skin.

c) Between 1941 and 1945, it has been estimated that the Nazis murdered six million Jews.

d) Free topic (you choose).

7 Individual study

Before the next class, prepare a short talk on a topic of your own choosing, in which you actively use some of the impact-generating techniques covered in this unit.

End of Unit Checklist

You have now completed Unit 4. Read through the statements below and make a record of your progress by ticking the most appropriate boxes.

5 = I feel very confident about this.

4 = I feel confident about this.

3 = I feel quite confident about this.

2 = I don't feel very confident about this.

1 = I still don't understand this at all.

For anything that you rate as a 2 or a 1, go back to that part of the unit and look at the material again.

	5	4	3	2	1
I know some alternative ways of opening an oral presentation.					
I know how to use word stress to achieve greater impact when I speak.					
I know what rhetorical questions are and how to use them effectively.					
I know how to use adverbs of degree for giving what I say more impact.					
I know how to use two different types of repetition as a technique for getting the audience's attention.					
I know how to apply the rule of threes.					
I know how my voice works and can apply some techniques for improving my voice projection.					
I know how to present numbers and data in a way that can create more impact.					

Unit 5 Using Visual Aids

In this unit, you will be looking at the following:

- Reasons for using visual aids
- Key features of effective visual aids
- Referencing academic sources
- Referring to visual aids
- Connected speech

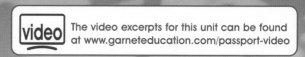

video The video excerpts for this unit can be found at www.garneteducation.com/passport-video

1 Reasons for using visual aids

1.1 Why is it helpful to use visual aids during an oral presentation? Discuss with a partner and make a list of your ideas in the space below.

_____

_____

_____

_____

_____

_____

_____

_____

1.2 A and B are examples of visual aids that two different students have prepared for a presentation about ways to improve their English. Which do you think is the most effective? Why?

Visual Aid A

Things that you can do to improve your ability in English:

- It is important to study regularly.
- You should make friends with native speakers because then you'll speak English more often.
- Reading English newspapers helps to develop your vocabulary.
- If you watch English TV and listen to English radio, you can pick up lots of idiomatic language.

Visual Aid B

Ways to improve your English:

- study regularly
- make native-speaker friends
- read English newspapers
- watch English TV
- listen to English radio

2 Key features of effective visual aids: Good titles

Visual aids need to have good titles. A good title helps to focus the audience's attention and prepares them for what the speaker is going to say.

2.1 Rewrite items *b–e* below to make them more effective as titles for a visual aid. An example has been done to help you.

Example
a) Reasons commonly given to explain why the climate is changing

_____

b) The economic advantages of doing business internationally

_____

c) People who have seen the Loch Ness monster

_____

d) Difficulties that international students typically experience

_____

e) Some of the ways in which culture can have an effect on advertising

_____

2.2 What are some common features of effective titles? Discuss with a partner.

2.3 Write the title for a visual aid that you might use in a presentation for your own subject area.

3 Key features of effective visual aids: Learn to KISS

Visual aids are not effective if they include too much information, so you should **Keep It Short and Simple [KISS]**. In Exercise 1.2, Visual Aid B is much better than Visual Aid A because its content only acts as a starting point – in other words, the audience still has a reason to listen to the speaker.

3.1 Create a visual aid about ways that students can save money by applying the KISS technique to the information on saving tips for students on the next page.

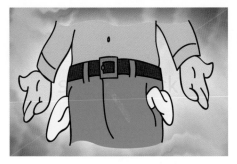 

Saving tips for students

While you are at university, and maybe even right after you graduate, you are going to be operating on a tight financial budget. However, there are a number of ways that you can save yourself money. The first thing you should do is to stop buying things that you don't really need. Impulse shopping can be very tempting, but the problem is that you end up blowing money on things that are 'nice to have' rather than things you 'need to have'. Before making any purchase, make sure that it is truly necessary.

Another thing you can do is to minimize your use of credit cards. Many students give in to the temptation to buy now and pay later, but unfortunately, spending habits like these can come back to haunt you. If you find that you can't use your credit card responsibly, hide it until you learn a little restraint, or better still, don't sign up for a credit card in the first place.

After paying for their accommodation and food, the next biggest drain on most students' finances is what they do for entertainment. Buying CDs and renting movies can easily gobble up lots of cash. The trick here is to check out your nearest public library. Many libraries offer their members the chance to take out DVDs, CDs and other forms of entertainment free of charge. By taking advantage of this resource, you can really reduce your entertainment costs.

Last but not least, we all know that everyone has at least one bad habit. Maybe you smoke, drink or buy yourself an expensive coffee every day in between lectures. Whatever your most expensive habit is, cut it out and you'll be amazed at just how much money you can save.

Schweitzer, K. (2007). 10 easy ways for students to save money. Retrieved March 20, 2008, from http://businessmajors.about.com/od/studentfinances/a/SaveMoney.htm

4 Key features of effective visual aids: Parallel writing

In Exercise 1.2, another reason why Visual Aid B is better than Visual Aid A is because it organizes its content using the technique of parallel writing. This means that your visual aid is the same throughout, i.e., you should use the same format, style and grammar for each point or slide.

4.1   Improve Visual Aid A by rewriting the content using parallel writing.

Visual Aid A

Ways to improve your health:

- it is important to drink lots of water

- you should eat plenty of fruit and vegetables

- regular exercise

- you shouldn't have too much salt

- getting 6–8 hours' sleep each night

Improved Visual Aid A

Ways to improve your health:

-
-
-
-
-

4.2   Create a visual aid that you might use in your own subject area using parallel writing to organize the content.

5 Referencing academic sources

In Unit 2, you learnt how to *orally* acknowledge any academic sources that you might have used in preparing your presentation. However, it is also important to acknowledge all academic sources *in writing*.

This can be done in the form of a bibliography handout that you distribute to your audience, or more typically, as a slide that you show at the very end of your presentation.

5.1 Look at the example presentation slide below, and discuss the following questions with a partner.

   a) What are the academic conventions used when referencing:
   • books?
   • journal articles?
   • online articles?

   b) What about the overall order in which academic sources should be listed?

References

Adams, T. (2012). Exploring international student beliefs about studying English. *Educational Review, 21,* 80–98.

Arnott, W. (2005). Coping Strategies of Exchange Students. *Journal of Educational Development, 40,* 23–30.

Barnes, J., & Hampton, Y. (2007). *Research Perspectives on International Student Mobility.* Oxford: Oxford University Press.

Bennett, H. (2000). The dark art of crossing educational cultures – do international students sink or swim? Retrieved 26.05.2012 from http://www.educationmatters.org.uk/articles/bennett.htm

Dobson, M. (2011). Does pre-departure cross-cultural training make a difference to the experience of international students? *Higher Education Review, 140,* 95–110.

Zachary, P. (2012). It's all about being critical – a contrastive analysis of different academic practices. *The Practical Teacher, 58,* 20–25.

5.2 Prepare an academic references slide based on the information in the table below.

Author	Type & name of academic source	Publication date	Publisher / Location of source
Fred Carter	ARTICLE Experiences of international students in the UK	2008	*Higher Education Review, 120,* 80–93.
Robert Stevens	BOOK The culture puzzle	2011	Cambridge: Cambridge University Press.
Sally Higgins	ELECTRONIC ARTICLE What do we mean by studying effectively?	2006	http://www.studyweb.com
Peter Smith & Tony Wilson	ARTICLE Learning to learn: What the latest research tells us.	2009	*Journal of Teaching Theory & Practice, 23,* 90–95.
Gwen Chatham	BOOK Getting the most out of university	2001	Oxford: Oxford University Press.

6 Referring to visual aids

Even if a visual aid has been designed using the techniques discussed in this unit, it can only work well if the presenter knows how to refer to it effectively.

6.1 🎧26 You will hear three short excerpts from a presentation in which the speaker refers to a visual aid about international student recruitment. The visual aid itself and the transcript of each excerpt are shown below. As you listen, fill in the blanks to complete the missing words.

Excerpt 1

As I mentioned earlier, this year we've seen a considerable increase in our international student memberships. _____ which countries these students are coming from and which clubs and societies they're choosing to join.

Excerpt 2

_____ the international students currently studying at the university. _____ the number of students and _____ their country of origin. _____, most international students are coming from four key areas: China, Japan, Nigeria and India.

Excerpt 3

_____, the university Travel Club is still the most popular society for international students, particularly for students from China and Nigeria. _____ _____ two other societies: the student Debating Group and the Drama Circle. _____ _____, the student Debating Group is a popular choice with Indian students, and the Drama Circle attracts lots of members from Japan.

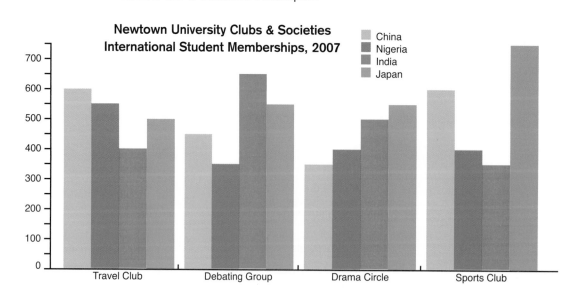

Newtown University Clubs & Societies International Student Memberships, 2007

Legend: China, Nigeria, India, Japan

Categories: Travel Club, Debating Group, Drama Circle, Sports Club

6.2 Some useful language for dealing with visual aids is listed in the Language focus box on the next page. Working with a partner, take turns using relevant phrases to practise referring to the Newtown Campus visual.

Referring to visual aids

Preparing the audience for a visual aid
a So now let's look at ...
b Now I'd like to show you ...

Explaining the purpose of a visual aid
c This graph / table / diagram shows ...
d This graph / table / diagram provides an overview of ...

Drawing attention to key features
e I would like to draw your attention to ...
f As you can see, the column on the left shows ...
g The columns on the right show ...
h The points in bold represent ...
i As this data indicates, ...

6.3 🎧27 Now use appropriate phrases from Language focus 11 to refer to the visual aid below. Compare what you say with the recording.

How international students spend their leisure time (Survey of 200 students, Newtown University, 2007)						
Students' country of origin	Shopping	Playing sports	Cooking	Cinema	Playing computer games	Meeting friends
China	5	15	20	5	**35**	20
Japan	**30**	5	6	12	4	18
Nigeria	10	**20**	7	2	4	14
India	8	5	16	10	2	**40**

7 Connected speech

International students often complain that native English speakers speak too quickly for them to follow. What they really mean is that native speakers tend to run different speech sounds together and make less of a distinction between individual words. It is important to be aware of the different ways that native speakers link sounds and words in rapid speech.

7.1 🎧28 Listen to the recording of items *a–d*. In each case, underline any words that the speaker runs together instead of pronouncing them completely separately.

a) We should have started recruiting in Asia much earlier.
b) One of the new doctorate students arrived last week.
c) He came with his wife and kids.
d) Have you met him yet?

7.2 🎧**29** Some typical features of English sound linking are detailed below. In each case, see if you can add one more example, then listen to the recordings and repeat.

   a) Consonants are often linked with vowels when the first word ends with a consonant sound and the second word begins with a vowel sound.

      Example:
      He's a*n* actor. (sounds like *heeza nacta*)

   b) When the /t/ sound appears between two consonant sounds, it often disappears completely.

      Example:
      He's coming nex*t* week. (sounds like *nex week*)

   c) When a word ends with a consonant sound and the following word begins with the same consonant sound, the first sound is absorbed by the second.

      Example:
      That was the last time I saw him. (sounds like *las time*)

   d) When two vowels appear next to each other, other sounds may come between them to help make the transition smooth. In spoken English, these sounds are usually /j/, /w/.

      Examples:
      She *i*sn't one of my students. (sounds like *she **y**isn't*)
      He went t*o u*nload his car. (sounds like *to **w**unload*)
      Australi*a i*s warmer than Britain. (sounds like *Australia **r**iz*)

7.3 🎧**30** It is less important for learners to be able to use these features themselves than it is to recognize them. You do not need to sound exactly like a native speaker, but you should aim for clear and comprehensible English. However, it can be useful to practise linking sounds and words if you want to sound more fluent.

Practise saying items *a–d* aloud and then compare yourself with the recording.

   a) She needs to ask his permission.
   b) He was an officer in the army.
   c) Just stay there for a moment.
   d) It's a bit tight.

Oral presentation top tip 5
Using visuals effectively

There is a common English saying that 'a picture is worth a thousand words', and students should keep this in mind when they are giving oral presentations. Information presented visually often has a greater impact and can be understood much more easily than information covered by a verbal explanation alone.

However, visual aids should be seen as just that, i.e., something designed to *support* a presentation visually. They should never become a presentation substitute. This is particularly true when using modern software packages such as Microsoft PowerPoint. Tools like these can help in producing professional-looking slide presentations, but it is easy to spend too much time working on the slides themselves and not enough time thinking about *how* they are going to be used or whether or not they are even appropriate. Remember: the same dos and don'ts apply to PowerPoint slides as to any other form of visual aid.

Some dos and don'ts of using visuals

 Do ask yourself the question: Is a visual aid necessary here? Could you achieve the same or even greater impact by doing something different, e.g., giving the audience a handout?

 Do make sure that your visual is written in a font big enough for everyone to see. Before you give your presentation, have a trial run in which you look at your visual from the back of the room – is the information still visible?

 Do check your visual for spelling mistakes and other formatting errors. The audience will be much less forgiving of mistakes that they can see.

 Do make sure that your body or shadow isn't blocking the visual while you are presenting. Be aware of where you are standing in relation to the visual.

 Don't talk to the visual. Remember that to keep the audience's attention, you must make frequent eye contact with them.

 Don't try to put too much information on a visual in one go. Use blank space well.

 Don't use graphics, animation or sound effects with PowerPoint slides unless they are particularly suitable for your presentation content. Always ask yourself: Am I adding to or detracting from the impact of what I want to present?

 Don't simply read the content of a visual aid to your audience. You should talk around the information rather than reading it out word for word.

By thinking carefully about the design of your visuals, along with when and how you are actually going to use them, you can really improve your presentation performance.

End of Unit Checklist

You have now completed Unit 5. Read through the statements below and make a record of your progress by ticking the most appropriate boxes.

5 = I feel very confident about this.

4 = I feel confident about this.

3 = I feel quite confident about this.

2 = I don't feel very confident about this.

1 = I still don't understand this at all.

For anything that you rate as a 2 or a 1, go back to that part of the unit and look at the material again.

	5	4	3	2	1
I know why visual aids can be helpful in a presentation.					
I know how to write effective titles for visual aids.					
I know how to KISS my visual aids so that they don't include too much information.					
I know how to use parallel writing to give the content of my visual aids more impact.					
I know how to prepare an audience for visual aids and how to explain their purpose.					
I know how to reference academic sources appropriately.					
I know some phrases for drawing attention to key features in visual aids.					
I know some different features of English connected speech.					
I know how to use visual aids effectively (Dos) and how to avoid some common mistakes (Don'ts).					

Unit 6 Giving Persuasive Presentations

In this unit, you will be looking at the following:

- Strategies used in persuading
- Examples of persuasive presentations
- Persuading versus informing
- Giving reasons and building arguments

video The video excerpts for this unit can be found at www.garneteducation.com/passport-video

The video excerpts for this unit can be found at www.garneteducation.com/passport-video

1 Strategies used in persuading

1.1 When was the last time that you persuaded someone to do something? Were you successful? Why/why not? Think about the role of language in the success or failure. Prepare to share your ideas with the rest of the class.

1.2 Work with a partner. You are going to role-play a situation where you try to persuade your partner to do something. Read the instructions below to prepare for a discussion with your partner. Make use of your conclusions from the discussion in Exercise 1.1 in your preparation.

Student A: Read the information in the report on page 58 and use it to help you prepare the opening for a persuasive presentation. Your goal is to persuade people not to waste water. Try out your presentation with your partner.

Student B: Read the report on page 58. Based on the information in this report, build an argument in favour of raising the current taxes on water. Try to persuade the person sitting next to you.

1.3 Think about the activity you have just completed. What strategy was your partner using to try and persuade you to do what he/she wanted? Was it effective? Why/why not? If not, what might have worked better?

1.4 Read the statements on the next page and mark on a scale of 1 to 5 how important you think they are. Prepare to explain the reasons for your choices.

1 = not important at all
2 = might be important sometimes
3 = important
4 = very important
5 = extremely important

	1	2	3	4	5
Before giving a persuasive presentation, you must be very clear what your objectives are. You should have specific goals.					
Before giving a persuasive presentation, you must think hard about your audience. You should decide what they probably already know and anticipate any barriers they might have.					
In a persuasive presentation, you should especially work on motivating your audience and arousing their interest.					
In a persuasive presentation, you must use a professional package such as PowerPoint.					
In a persuasive presentation, you must dress in formal clothes.					
In a persuasive presentation, you should argue your case by appealing to the audience's emotions.					
In a persuasive presentation, you should argue your case by using facts.					
In a persuasive presentation, you should keep to your position and not modify your ideas.					

2 Examples of persuasive presentations

2.1 Below are four typical situations when you might be asked to give a persuasive presentation. Can you add any other examples? For instance, when might you have to give a persuasive presentation in your own academic subject area?

a) IT: Students have been asked to compare three different programs and decide which one they think is the best for a particular application.
b) Law: Students have been asked to argue a case.
c) Business: Students have been asked to present their ideas for a marketing plan.
d) Architecture: Students have been asked to defend various types of building design and propose which one they think is the most effective.

3   Persuading versus informing

We looked at the general structure of oral presentations in Unit 1. However, there are some important differences between informative presentations and persuasive presentations.

3.1   🎧 **31** You are going to hear two openings for a presentation about the same general topic. Make a note of any differences that you notice. Which opening is the most persuasive? Why?

_____

_____

_____

_____

_____

_____

_____

_____

3.2   🎧 **32** Now listen to the conclusions of the presentations from Exercise 3.1. Once again, make a note of any differences that you notice.

_____

_____

_____

_____

_____

_____

_____

_____

3.3   Compare your ideas with the ones in the table on the next page.

Informative presentations

General introduction
The speaker introduces him/herself.

The overview
The speaker tells the audience what the topic of the presentation will be. The main focus is on sharing information.

'In my presentation today, I'm going to talk about cycling to the campus rather than coming by car.'

The body
The speaker talks about the presentation topic in detail. The content is neutral, with a focus on sharing information.

The conclusion
The speaker lets the audience know that he/she is about to finish.

'That brings us to the end of my presentation today. Thank you very much for listening. If anyone has any questions, I'd be happy to answer them.'

The chance for discussion
The speaker gives the audience the opportunity to ask questions.

Persuasive presentations

General introduction
The speaker introduces him/herself.

The overview
The speaker tells the audience what the topic of the presentation will be. The main focus is on achieving a particular objective.

'In my presentation today, I'm going to focus on why I strongly believe that more people should be cycling to the campus rather than coming by car.'

The body
The speaker talks about the presentation topic in detail. The content is strategic, with a focus on giving reasons and building arguments (see Exercise 4).

The conclusion
The speaker lets the audience know that he/she is about to finish. The speaker reminds the audience of his/her main objective.

'That brings us to the end of my presentation today. As I'm sure you'll now agree, travelling to the campus by bicycle can offer you a number of distinct advantages, not only in terms of helping the environment, but also in terms of saving you money and raising the level of your personal safety. Thank you very much for listening. If anyone has any questions, I'd be happy to answer them.'

The chance for discussion
The speaker gives the audience the opportunity to ask questions.

3.4 Prepare a persuasive presentation opening and conclusion on one of the topics below:

   a) being a vegetarian
   b) exercising regularly
   c) extending the university library opening hours
   d) using Macintosh computers instead of PCs
   e) free topic (you choose)

4   Giving reasons and building arguments

In order to persuade people, in the body of your presentation you must be able to state your opinions and then support them by giving reasons and building convincing arguments.

4.1 🎧**33** Listen to an excerpt from a presentation in which the speaker tries to persuade the audience that British policemen shouldn't carry guns. What specific reasons does the speaker put forward to support this opinion?

4.2 🎧**33** The presenter uses two particular techniques to help him build his arguments. These are listed below. Listen to the presentation excerpt again and try to make a note of the language he uses in each technique.

Technique A:

Making a statement and then listing the supporting points in a sequence.

_____

_____

_____

_____

_____

_____

Technique B:

Introducing a typical opposing argument, but then giving an answer to it or explaining why it is not a valid argument.

_____

_____

_____

_____

4.3 Choose one of the topics *b–f* below. Give your opinion and prepare a persuasive argument using techniques A and B. An example has been done to help you. You can also look at the examples in Language focus 12 below.

a) Example topic:
Smoking on campus

Example argument:

I strongly believe that smoking on campus should only be allowed in clearly marked areas. Aside from the fact that smokers are potentially damaging the health of the people around them, there's also the issue of fire safety. The fire alarms went off five times last month, and in each case, it was thought to be due to careless smokers.

But maybe some of you are thinking, what about individual rights? Well, I'm not suggesting that people shouldn't have the right to smoke; obviously, they should. All I'm saying is that they should smoke in an area that doesn't affect other people.

b) 24-hour licensing laws
c) Internet censorship
d) gun ownership
e) animal experimentation
f) free topic (you choose)

Language focus 12

Techniques for building arguments

Listing supporting points in sequential order
a Aside from the fact that ..., there's also the issue of ...
b For one thing, ...; for another ...
c First of all ...; second ...; third ...
d On the one hand ...; on the other ...

Introducing a typical opposing argument
e But maybe some of you are thinking, what about ...?
f Of course, the usual response is ...
g Some people would say ...

Refuting an opposing argument with a counterargument
h But I'm not suggesting ... All I'm saying is ...
i Actually, all the evidence shows ...
j In fact, the opposite is true. In my experience ...

4.4 Prepare a 15- to 20-minute persuasive presentation on a topic of your own choosing. Make sure that you structure your information appropriately and that you use some of the language and techniques covered in this unit.

Oral presentation top tip 6
Speaking from note cards

If you are worried about forgetting your presentation content, one thing you can do is to make yourself a set of note cards. Note cards can be very helpful for public speakers, because they can serve as a reminder of the presentation structure and help to keep it on track. This is especially true for speakers not using presentation slides such as PowerPoint.

As well as the presentation content, note cards can also include reminders about the delivery, e.g., when to ask for questions; when to pause; when to tell a joke. Two example note cards are shown below.

1 Introduction
How many of you here regularly eat junk food?

[Ask for a show of hands]

5 Conclusion
More fruit and vegetables is better for your health.

[Ask for questions]

Some dos and don'ts of using note cards

☑☺ **Do** keep the writing on your note cards to an absolute minimum. The cards should only be a reminder of what you want to talk about next.

☑☺ **Do** use only one side of each note card.

☑☺ **Do** make sure that you write on your cards clearly. If your handwriting is really bad, print or type. It is also a good idea to use colour coding for the different parts.

☑☺ **Do** make sure that your cards are in the right order and number them carefully. It can be helpful to punch a hole in the top corner of your note cards and thread them onto a key ring. That way, if you accidentally drop your cards, at least you'll be able to find your place again easily.

☒☹ **Don't** just talk to your cards. Remember that to keep the audience's attention, you must make frequent eye contact with them.

☒☹ **Don't** try to use too many cards.

Text for Exercise 1.2

Read through the information below and use it to help you prepare the opening for a persuasive presentation. Your goal is to persuade people not to waste water.

Averting a water crisis

If current trends in water policy and investment hold or worsen, we will soon face threats to the global food supply, further environmental damage and ongoing health risks for the hundreds of millions of people lacking access to clean water. These findings come from *Global Water Outlook to 2025: Averting an Impending Crisis*, a report by the International Food Policy Research Institute (IFPRI) and the International Water Management Institute (IWMI) released on World Food Day. Using sophisticated computer modelling, the report projects that by 2025, water scarcity will cause annual global losses of 350 million metric tons of food production – slightly more than the entire current US grain crop.

'Unless we change policies and priorities, in 20 years there won't be enough water for cities, households, the environment or growing food,' cautioned Dr Mark Rosegrant, lead author of the report and senior research fellow at IFPRI. 'Water is not like oil. There is no substitute. If we continue to take it for granted, much of the earth is going to run short of water or food – or both.'

Due in part to rapid population growth and urbanization in developing countries, water use for households, industry and agriculture will increase by at least 50 per cent in the next 20 years. Increased competition for water will severely limit the availability of water for irrigation, which in turn will seriously constrain the world's production of food.

Declines in food supply could cause prices to skyrocket, and higher prices will lead to significant increases in malnutrition, since many poor people in developing countries already spend more than half their income on food.

'For hundreds of millions of poor farmers in developing countries, a lack of access to water for growing food is the most important constraint they face,' said Frank Rijsberman, director general of IWMI. 'If countries continue to underinvest in building strong institutions and policies to support water governance and approaches to give better access to water to poor communities, growth rates for crop yields will fall worldwide in the next 25 years, primarily because of water scarcity.'

According to the report, it would take only a moderate worsening in global water policy to bring about a genuine water crisis. If governments continue to cut spending on crop research, technology and infrastructure, while failing to implement institutional and management reforms, global grain production will drop by ten per cent over business-as-usual levels, equivalent to losing the entire annual grain crop of India.

Fundamental changes in water policies and investment priorities could achieve substantial benefits and sustainable use of water. For example, the report recommends pricing water to reflect its cost and value.

'Although water subsidies are commonplace in developing countries, they tend to benefit relatively wealthy people,' explained Dr Peter Hazell, director of Environment and Production Technology at IFPRI. 'Making affluent people pay for water would encourage them to conserve. It would also free up financial resources to provide clean, safe water to poor people.'

The report also recommends increased investment in crop research, technological change and rural infrastructure to boost water productivity and growth of crop yields in rain-fed farming, which will account for half the increase in food production between 1995 and 2025.

Source: International Food Policy Research Institute. 2002. *New report projects impending water crisis, solutions to avert it*. Press release, October 16. Washington, D.C.: International Food Policy Research Institute.

End of Unit Checklist

You have now completed Unit 6. Read through the statements below and make a record of your progress by ticking the most appropriate boxes.

5 = I feel very confident about this.

4 = I feel confident about this.

3 = I feel quite confident about this.

2 = I don't feel very confident about this.

1 = I still don't understand this at all.

For anything that you rate as a 2 or a 1, go back to that part of the unit and look at the material again.

	5	4	3	2	1
I know some different strategies for persuading people.					
I know when I might be required to give a persuasive presentation for my studies/in the workplace.					
I know what the main differences are between informative and persuasive presentations.					
I know how to use two different techniques for giving reasons and building arguments.					
I know some key language for giving reasons and building arguments.					
I know how to use note cards effectively (Dos) and how to avoid some common mistakes (Don'ts).					

Review Unit

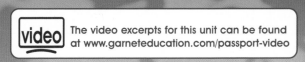

1   Oral presentation format and structure (Units 1–3)

1.1   🎧 **34** Listen to the opening of an informative oral presentation and make a note of the following:

  a) what the presentation will be about.
  b) how many parts the presentation will be in.

1.2   🎧 **35** Now listen to the presentation body. As you listen, make notes.

1.3   Use your notes to check your comprehension by answering questions a–o.

  a) According to the presenter, how was water first created?
  b) By what process were the oceans and seas formed?
  c) Where is most of the Earth's water stored?
  d) What is meant by the terms 'aeration zone' and 'saturation zone'?
  e) What surprising fact does the presenter give about the Sahara Desert?
  f) Where does most of the Earth's rainfall go?
  g) What is 'surface tension' and how does it work?
  h) What unique property does water have with regard to heat?
  i) What unique property does water have with regard to cold?
  j) What important role do ice floes play in the Arctic? Why is this critical for the future of the planet?
  k) What is the Challenger Deep and where is it located?
  l) Why do creatures living at the bottom of the Hudson Canyon need to be highly specialized?
  m) What is the Gulf Stream?
  n) What causes tides to fall and rise?
  o) What is the difference between a Spring tide and a Neap tide?

1.4   🎧 **36** Listen to the very end of the presentation. What three questions does the presenter get asked?

1.5   Now think of at least three questions (a 'Straight' question; a 'Give me more' question; and an 'I didn't understand, so tell me again' question) that you could ask the presenter yourself, if you were one of the audience. Practise asking these questions with your teacher.

2   Oral presentation delivery and style (Units 1–4)

2.1   🎧 **34** Listen to the presentation opening again and mark // on the transcript below to indicate all the places in which the speaker pauses.

Good morning everyone I think we'd better get started my name is Dr Steven Bishop thank you very much for coming along to my presentation today now for the next ten minutes or so I'm going to talk about a substance that we're all very familiar with and one that none of us can do without have you any idea as to what that might be?

2.2   Now imagine that *you* are Dr Steven Bishop. Practise delivering the presentation opening, making sure that you pause in all the same places.

2.3   What technique does Dr Bishop use to get the audience's attention in his opening? Do you think this is effective? Discuss with a partner.

2.4   Devise an *alternative* opening for this presentation using one of the other techniques for creating impact from Unit 4. Practise delivering your new opening as far as the lead-in stage.

2.5   Give items *b–e* below more impact by adding a rhetorical question, as in the example.

Example

a) When we're talking about water, it's important to remember that we're referring to a substance that has been used, purified and then reused for about 3,000 million years. The accepted scientific theory of how water was first created states that when the Earth was formed, a chemical reaction took place between the gases hydrogen and oxygen.

When we're talking about water, it's important to remember that we're referring to a substance that has been used, purified and then reused for about 3,000 million years. *But where did it all come from in the first place?* Well, the accepted scientific theory of how water was first created states that when the Earth was formed, a chemical reaction took place between the gases hydrogen and oxygen.

b) If we think about our water reserves and where our water is actually based, as you might expect, the bulk of the Earth's water, about 97.2 per cent of it, lies in the great oceans.

c) The atmosphere holds about 3,100 cubic miles of water – enough to cover the entire planet with one inch of rain if it all came down at the same time.

d) Only about ⅙ of the planet's total rainfall soaks into the ground.

e) Insects have this almost magical ability to walk on water – well, that comes down to water's surface tension.

2.6 🎧 **37** Items *a–e* below are all excerpts from the presentation about water. Listen carefully and underline the words that the speaker stresses the most. The first one has been done for you as an example.

a) So let's <u>start</u>, then, with <u>where</u> water <u>comes</u> from; its early <u>history</u>, if you like.

b) Now, the first point I'd like to make is that the Earth retains all of the water ever created.

c) The accepted scientific theory of how water was first created states that when the Earth was formed, a chemical reaction took place between the gases hydrogen and oxygen.

d) As the temperatures dropped, this layer of cloud released its water in a torrential downpour that lasted an amazing 60,000 years.

e) The truly remarkable thing is, the level of the oceans and the amount of water on the Earth has actually remained relatively stable ever since.

2.7 🎧 **38** Now listen to the recording of items *f–j*. Mark whether or not the speaker's intonation rises ↑ or falls ↓ on the words that are underlined.

f) The Earth's surface water is stored in <u>rivers</u>, <u>lakes</u>, <u>oceans</u> and <u>seas</u>.

g) Water floats when it's frozen, <u>doesn't it</u>?

h) Of course, water floats when it's frozen, <u>doesn't it</u>? That's why we have icebergs.

i) This brings us to the final part of my <u>presentation</u>.

j) Does anyone have any <u>questions</u>?

2.8 Work with a partner. Take turns reading items *a–d* aloud, paying particular attention to your intonation for the words that have been underlined.

a) Water in the saturation zone feeds <u>swamps</u>, <u>rivers</u>, <u>lakes</u> and <u>wells</u>.

b) When water boils, we can see bubbles bursting through the surface tension, <u>can't we</u>? That's the point when we know its temperature has reached 100 degrees.

c) Are the ice floes really that <u>important</u>?

d) The largest tides occur in places where the sea runs into <u>bottlenecks</u>.

2.9 🎧 **39** Now listen to the recording of items *a–d*. Was your intonation the same?

2.10 🎧 **40** Rewrite statements *b–d* below, giving them greater impact by adding an adverb of degree (look back at Unit 4 if you can't remember what this is). An example has been done to help you. Practise saying the new versions out loud, then compare yourself with the recording.

Example

a) The remarkable thing is that the level of the oceans has actually remained relatively stable ever since.

The **truly** remarkable thing is that the level of the oceans has actually remained relatively stable ever since.

_____

b) Most animals would find such living conditions intolerable.

_____

c) If the ice built up from the ocean beds, life as we currently know it would be unable to survive.

_____

d) Without surface tension, it would be impossible for insects to walk on water.

_____

2.11 🎧 **41** Rewrite statements *e–i* using strategic repetition and doubling techniques (again, look back at Unit 4 if you can't remember what these are) to add extra emphasis. Practise saying the rewritten statements out loud, then compare yourself with the recording.

e) There can be no doubt whatsoever that water is a very important substance.

_____

f) There are many cubic miles of water hidden beneath the Earth's surface.

_____

g) It is far easier for us to waste water than it is to save it.

_____

h) As you go deeper, the water pressure becomes greater.

_____

i) Once you get past a few thousand feet, it becomes harder for organisms to survive unless they're highly specialized.

_____

2.12 The presentation about water contains a lot of different numbers and data. Think of a way to present key facts *a* and *b*, so that the audience would be able to relate to the data easily and you could gain maximum impact.

a) The Hudson Canyon, just off the coast of New York, is 150 miles long.

b) The Gulf Stream is about 50 miles wide and up to 1,500 feet deep.

3 Using visual aids (Unit 5)

3.1 A transcript from the presentation about water is given below. Use this information to make a visual aid that could be shown at the beginning of the presentation to help the speaker explain the structure.

Basically, I'm going to talk about the substance H_2O, better known as water …
and to highlight the importance of this substance, the presentation is entitled: 'Water: Amazing Liquid of Life'. Now, I've divided my presentation into three parts. To start, I'm going to talk about where water comes from and where the Earth keeps most of its current reserves. Then, I'd like to focus on what I'll call 'the wonders of water' and give you some interesting facts about its physical properties. And to finish off, I'll say a little about some key features of our great oceans and seas.

3.2 Improve the visual aid below by applying the parallel writing technique.

	Some key properties of water
_____ _____ _____	• When it meets other materials, water forms a skin.
_____ _____ _____	• It can absorb more heat than any other common substance without experiencing a considerable rise in temperature.
_____ _____ _____	• Another one of water's wonders is that it floats when frozen.
_____ _____ _____	• Although water expands at freezing point, it actually becomes less dense.

3.3   Create a visual aid about the key features of our oceans and seas by applying the KISS technique to the information below.

When you look out over an ocean or sea, if you were actually able to see beneath the waves, you'd find a whole new world of spectacular canyons, great plains and enormous mountain ranges. One such mountain range, the Mid-Atlantic Ridge, runs for about 10,000 miles between Iceland and the Antarctic, which makes it the largest mountain range in the world. And in fact, believe it or not, Iceland, the Ascension Islands and the Azores are all just examples of this underwater mountain range's highest peaks.

Now, as well as great mountain ranges, our oceans also hide some extremely deep holes and trenches. The deepest known trench is the so-called 'Challenger Deep', situated off the island of Guam in the Pacific. This trench goes down for an amazing seven miles, and just to give you some idea of how deep that actually is, if we put Everest into it, there would *still* be about a mile of water above the summit. Surprising, isn't it?

Now, I said a moment ago, our oceans contain spectacular canyons. The Hudson Canyon, just off the coast of New York, is 150 miles long and 16,500 feet deep. Creatures living at the bottom of this canyon have to be able to cope with *tremendous* water pressure. And just to give you some idea of what I mean by that, at a depth of 13,000 feet, the water pressure is nearly three tons to the square foot, so if we're looking at a depth of over 16,000 feet, clearly only highly specialized organisms are able to survive; most animals would actually find such living conditions intolerable.

3.4   Imagine that you have been asked to give a presentation about water. Read through the information that follows and use it to help you refer to the visual aid on the right. Look back at Unit 5 if you are unsure of how to prepare the audience for a visual aid, explain its purpose and draw attention to key features.

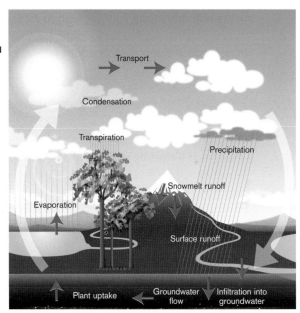

The hydrologic cycle, commonly known as 'the water cycle', consists of seven major processes: evaporation (water is converted to the gaseous state of water vapour); transpiration (evaporation of water from plants); condensation (water vapour is converted back into liquid water); precipitation (the falling of water in the form of rain, sleet, hail or snow); infiltration (water movement into the soil); percolation (the downward flow of water through soil to the aquifer); and runoff (surface movement of water back to a body of water to repeat the cycle; usually occurs down a sloping surface).

3.5   🎧 **42** Compare what you said with the recording.

Language Reference Section

A   Key phrases

Opening phrases (Unit 1)

In my presentation today, I'm going to look at *some of the issues affecting tourism in Thailand.*

In this presentation, I'll be describing *the main forms of cancer that we are currently finding in women over the age of 40.*

For the next ten minutes or so, I'd like to give you *some of the reasons why most modern historians think the First World War started.*

In my talk this morning, I'm going to focus on *three of Monet's paintings.*

In my presentation, I'll talk about *four key effects that acid rain is having on our environment.*

Phrases for giving an overview (Unit 1)

In my presentation today, I'm going to talk about *images of violence in the movies of Quentin Tarantino.* **I'll start by looking at** *'Pulp Fiction', arguably his best known-work.* **Next, I'll focus on** *'Reservoir Dogs'* **and to finish off, I'll consider** *'Kill Bill'.*

For the next 20 minutes or so, I'm going to look at *some of the different factors that have an impact on international communication.* **Basically, I've divided my presentation into three parts. In the first part, I'll talk about** *cultural values and the way that these determine human behaviour.* **Then, in the second part, I'll look at** *the way that linguistic differences have an impact on how we think and the way in which we express ourselves.* **And in the final part, I'll focus on** *non-verbal communication* **and consider** *the ways in which gestures, facial expressions and body posture can all transmit meaning just as effectively as words.*

Lead-in phrases (Unit 2)

So, for starters then, let's look at *cultural values.*

Right, to begin with, let's look at *cultural values.*

OK, let's start by looking at *cultural values.*

Linking phrases (Unit 2)

Now I'd like to move on to the next part of my presentation, which is *how Hitler got the support of the German people.*

Next, I'd like to look at my second point today: *some of the ways in which mobile phone technology has developed.*

This leads us to my next point: *suggestions for improving your English speaking.*

This brings us to the final part of my presentation today: *what countries can do to reduce their greenhouse gas emissions.*

Ending phrases (Unit 2)

That concludes my presentation. Are there any questions?

That brings us to the end of my presentation today. Thank you very much for listening. Does anyone have any questions?

Right then, as I hope to have shown this morning, it's clear that *Scotland has many attractions for foreign tourists.* **Now, does anyone have any questions?**

I hope you've enjoyed my presentation today. If anyone has any questions, I'll do my best to answer them.

Closing phrases (Unit 3)

Does anyone have any more questions? *[NO QUESTIONS]* **In that case, I'll finish my presentation here. Thank you for listening.**

If there are no more questions, I'll stop here. Thanks very much for your attention.

Alternative opening phrases (Unit 4)

Asking the audience a question:

Before I start my presentation today, I'd like to ask you all a question.
[QUESTION] **Put your hand up, please, if your answer is 'yes'.**

Good afternoon, everyone. Before we get started, I have a quick question.
[QUESTION] **Please raise your hand if the answer is 'yes'.**

Asking the audience to do something:

Before I start my presentation today, I'd like to carry out a small experiment. Can you stand up, please, if *you've had any junk food in the last week?*

Good morning, everyone. Before we get started, I have a little task for you. Can you stand up, please, if *you've had any junk food in the last week?*

Getting the audience's attention with some unexpected information:

Good afternoon, everyone. Before I start my presentation today, I'd like to share a few facts with you. As you probably all know, *Scotland has the highest mountain in the whole of the UK.* **You may also have heard that** *Scotland has the largest freshwater lake in the UK.* **But I wonder how many of you realize that, according to a recent survey,** *Scotland has the highest incidence of teenage obesity, not only in the UK but in all of Europe?*

Phrases for using visual aids (Unit 5)

Preparing the audience for a visual aid:

So now let's look at …
Now I'd like to show you …

Explaining the purpose of a visual aid:

This graph shows …
This table provides an overview of …

Drawing attention to key features:

I would like to draw your attention to …
As you can see, the column on the left shows …
The columns on the right show …
The points in bold represent …
As this data indicates, …

Phrases for building arguments (Unit 6)

Listing supporting points in sequential order:

Aside from the fact that …, there's also the issue of …
For one thing, … ; for another …
First of all …; second …; third …
On the one hand …; on the other …

Introducing a typical opposing argument:

But maybe some of you are thinking, what about …?
Of course, the usual response is …
Some people would say …

Refuting an opposing argument with a counterargument:

But I'm not suggesting … All I'm saying is …
Actually, all the evidence shows …
In fact, the opposite is true. In my experience …

B Presentation action verbs

Action verbs + no preposition

consider	I'll **consider** some of the main reasons behind global warming.
define	I'll **define** what is meant by existentialism.
describe	I'll **describe** three outcomes of their foreign policy.
explain	I'll **explain** why overpricing is causing a sharp decline in sales.
list	I'll **list** the main symptoms of HIV.
outline	I'll **outline** some key advantages of switching to gas.
propose	I'll **propose** a number of changes.
recommend	I'll **recommend** three new policies for our future development.
suggest	I'll **suggest** some practical solutions.

Action verbs + the preposition *about*

talk about	I'll **talk about** why diseases like malaria are on the increase.
tell (someone) about	I'll **tell** you **about** the three most popular tourist destinations.

Action verbs + the preposition *on*

concentrate on	I'll **concentrate on** what the government should be doing.
focus on	I'll **focus on** how companies can become more green.

Action verbs + the preposition *at*

look at	I'll **look at** the reasons behind the invasion.

C Common verb tenses

The future with *will*

- Used in the presentation overview stage to explain future intentions:
  *In my presentation this morning, **I'll talk about** the main causes of global warming.*

- Used in the final stage to end the presentation:
  *If there are no more questions, then **I'll end** my presentation here. Thanks for listening.*

The future with *going to*

- Used in the presentation overview stage to explain future intentions:
  *In my presentation this morning, **I'm going to talk about** the main causes of global warming.*

- Used in the presentation body to link different sections:
  *Now, **I'm going to move on to** the second part of my presentation today: the effects of global warming.*

The future continuous

- Used in the presentation overview stage to explain future intentions:
  *In my presentation this morning, **I'll be talking about** the main causes of global warming.*

The conditional form – *I'd like to*

- Used in the presentation overview stage to explain future intentions:
  *In my presentation this morning, **I'd like to focus on** the main causes of global warming.*

- Used in the presentation body to link different sections:
  *Now, **I'd like to move on to** the second part of my presentation today: the effects of global warming.*

The present simple

- Used in the closing stage to finish the presentation off:
  *That **concludes** my presentation today. Thank you very much for listening.*
  *That **brings us to the end of** my presentation today. Thanks for your attention.*

D   Intonation patterns

Rising intonation

- To indicate a question:

  Why not use a <u>submarine</u>?

- For the first few items in a list:

  The surface water is stored in <u>rivers</u>, <u>lakes</u>, <u>oceans</u> ….

- In tag questions when the speaker is unsure about something:

  Water boils at 100 degrees centigrade, <u>doesn't it</u>?

Falling intonation

- To indicate that something is finishing:

  That brings us to the end of my presentation <u>today</u>.

- For the last item in a list:

  The surface water is stored in rivers, lakes, oceans and <u>seas</u>.

- In tag questions when the speaker is sure of something:

  Water floats when frozen, <u>doesn't it</u>? That's why we have icebergs.

Falling-rising intonation

- To indicate uncertainty:

The Loch Ness monster may just be a large fish.

It's possible that the witnesses were simply mistaken.

E Features of connected speech

Consonants are often linked with vowels when the first word ends with a consonant sound and the second word begins with a vowel sound.

- *She's an actress. [sounds like sheeza nactress]*

When the /t/ sound appears between two consonant sounds, it often disappears completely.

- They're coming nex(t) week. *[sounds like nex week]*

When a word ends with a consonant sound and the following word begins with the same consonant sound, the first sound is absorbed by the second.

- She's a big girl. *[sounds like bi girl]*

When two vowels appear next to each other, other sounds may come between them to help make the transition smooth. In spoken English, these sounds are usually /y/, /w/ and /r/.

- He isn't working here. *[sounds like he yisn't]*

- They wanted to unload the truck. *[sounds like to wunload]*

- Bolivia is in South America. *[sounds like Bolivia riz]*

Audio CD and Video Transcript

video The video excerpts can be found at www.garneteducation.com/passport-video

Unit 1
Track 1: Presentation openings: Exercise 3.1

Presentation 1

Hi, everyone. As you know, my name is Ichiko Howells and I come from Japan. In my seminar presentation today, I am going to talk about some of the cultural differences between Japan and the UK.

Presentation 2

I'd just like to start by saying it's a great pleasure to be presenting at this symposium. My name is Professor Paul Baxter and I work at the Business School at the University of Aberdeen. For the next hour or so, I'd like to explain how American cultural values influence their television advertising …

Track 2: Presentation structure: Exercise 4.1

Presentation 1

Good morning, everyone. In my seminar presentation today, I'm going to talk about the poetry of Philip Larkin. Basically, I've divided my talk into three parts. In the first part, I'll look at Larkin's first collection of poems, *The North Ship*. Next, I'll focus on what was probably his most famous book, *The Whitsun Weddings*. And finally, I'll tell you about his last published anthology, *High Windows*.

Presentation 2

Right, for the next 30 minutes or so, I'd like to tell you about one of my favourite British writers, Jane Austen. In the first part of the presentation, I'll look at Austen's upbringing and some of the things that may have had an influence on her writing. Then, I'll move on specifically to talk about one of her most famous works, *Pride and Prejudice*.

Track 3: Giving an overview: Exercise 4.4

Presentation 1

In my presentation this morning, I'm going to talk about typical London tourist attractions. I'll start by looking at Buckingham Palace, arguably the most popular attraction for tourists. Next, I'll focus on the British Museum, and to finish off, I'll consider the Tower of London.

Presentation 2

For the next 20 minutes or so, I'm going to look at some of the different effects of global warming. Basically, I've divided my presentation into three parts. In the first part, I'll talk about the melting glaciers and the way that these are contributing to rising sea levels. Then, in the second part, I'll look at climate change and give you some examples of how this is having a serious impact on wild animals' behaviour and habitat. And in the final part, I'll focus on the retreating snowlines and consider how these are causing the death of certain species of trees.

Track 4: Speaking effectively: Exercise 5.1

For the next 20 minutes or so // I'm going to look at some of the different effects of global warming // Basically // I've divided my presentation into three parts // In the first part // I'll talk about the melting glaciers / and the way that these are contributing to rising sea levels // Then // in the second part // I'll look at climate change // and give you some examples of how this is having a serious impact on wild animals' behaviour // and habitat // And in the final part // I'll focus on the retreating snowlines // and consider how these are causing the death // of certain species of trees.

Unit 2
Track 5: Leading in to a presentation: Exercise 2.1

In my presentation this morning, I'm going to talk about some famous British inventors and the products that they have developed. Basically, I've divided this presentation into three parts. In the first part, I'll talk about Alexander Graham Bell and the invention of the telephone. Then, in the second part, I'll look at the work of John Logie Baird and his development of the television. And to finish off, I'll discuss Alexander Fleming and his research on the antibiotic we now know as penicillin. So, let's start by looking at …

Track 6: Presentation about the IELTS exam: Exercise 3.1

Good morning, everyone, and welcome to the Fair. It's a real pleasure to see so many of you here taking part. My name is Lisa Thompson and I'm a senior manager at the British Council here in Hong Kong. As I think you know, we hold this Information Fair every year for Hong Kong students planning to study in the UK. And in this first presentation today, I'm going to talk about the most common English-language entry qualification recognized by British universities – the International English Language Testing System, perhaps better known to you as the 'IELTS' examination.

I have divided my presentation into four parts. I will start by looking at the history of IELTS and give you some background. Then, in the second part, I'll give you an overview of the examination format and look at how the different skills are actually tested. In Part 3, I'll be focusing on IELTS scores and what they mean. And finally, in the last part of my presentation today, I'll say a little bit about the problems that we can have with IELTS.

So, let's start then by looking at the history and background of IELTS. The test was first developed in 1989 and its purpose, as I am sure you all know, was and indeed still is, to measure a student's ability to communicate in English when their ultimate goal is to study or work where English is the main language of communication … (FADE OUT)

Now I'd like to move on to the second part of my presentation today, the IELTS examination format. As I mentioned earlier, the exam aims to test each of the four skills, and this is reflected in the format of the paper. Students taking the IELTS exam first sit papers in listening, reading and writing – these must be completed in one day – and they then have a speaking paper in the form of a short interview. However, what you may not know is that there are actually two different versions of IELTS – a test for General English and a test for Academic English … (FADE OUT)

This leads us to my third point – how to interpret IELTS scores. IELTS scores are based on nine different headings, ranging from Expert Users in Band 9 down to Non-Users in Band 1. The different scores for each separate component are added together to make a final total. For most British colleges and universities, the critical IELTS bands are between 6 and 7, as these are the ones which measure whether or not a student can join a course directly, without having to go through an English Language Foundation Programme … (FADE OUT)

Now I would like to move on to the final part of my presentation today to talk about some of the problems with IELTS …(FADE OUT)

Track 7: Lead-in phrases: Exercise 4.1

a) OK, let's start by looking at where paper was actually invented.
b) So, for starters, let's look at the history of the telephone.
c) Now I'd like to move on to the next part of my presentation, which is how Hitler got the support of the German people.
d) Next, I'd like to look at my second point today: some of the ways in which mobile phone technology has developed.
e) This leads us to my next point: suggestions for improving your English speaking.
f) Right, I'm going to finish off today by looking at Alexander Fleming and the antibiotic penicillin.
g) This brings us to the final part of my presentation today: what countries can do to reduce their greenhouse gas emissions.

Unit 3
Track 8: Presentation about the Loch Ness monster: Exercise 1.2

Good morning, everyone, it's really wonderful to see so many people here. My name's Paul Harris and I have the truly great honour of opening this most unconventional of conventions. I'm absolutely delighted to be here with you today.

Over the next two days, you're going to hear presentations and panel discussions on a broad range of topics related to the world of the paranormal and cryptozoology, ranging from UFOs in America to the Yeti in Tibet. But in this opening paper, I'd like to focus your attention on a long-standing mystery much closer to home. As I think some of you know already, I'm going to talk about the Loch Ness monster.

Now, I've divided my presentation into three main parts. In the first part, I'll say a little about the geography of Loch Ness and give you some background to the mystery. Then, in Part 2, I'll talk about some of the classic monster sightings. And finally, in Part 3, I'm going to try to answer the question: if there is such a thing as the Loch Ness monster, what on earth could it be?

So, to begin with, let's start by looking at the physical geography of the loch.

As most of you probably know, Loch Ness is situated in the highlands of Scotland, roughly about 600 miles from where we are today. It's a very big loch – about 24 miles long and between one

and one and a half miles wide – and it represents the largest volume of freshwater in the British Isles. Now, Loch Ness certainly isn't the deepest lake in Britain – that award actually goes to Loch Morar over on the west coast – but with an average depth of over 200 metres for most of its length, Loch Ness is still pretty deep and in fact, some statisticians have calculated that every man, woman and child on the planet could be submerged in Loch Ness and there'd still be room for mystery!

Now, hopefully that gives you some idea of where the loch is situated and its physical characteristics. As I said at the beginning though, I'd also like to talk about the background to the mystery. Although there have been reports of a strange animal in Loch Ness right back to the 6th century – there's even a record of Saint Columba encountering a water monster near Loch Ness in 565AD – the Loch Ness monster as we currently know it first came to the general public's attention back in 1933. A local couple called Mr and Mrs Mackay were travelling in a car by the side of the loch, when they saw a big disturbance in the water. Mr Mackay was driving, so he had to pay attention to the road, but his wife later said that in the middle of the water disturbance, she saw a big black hump. She realized that she was watching a living creature when this hump shot off to the other side of the loch, turned in half a circle and then suddenly sank. She and her husband waited to see if the animal would come up again, but it had gone. The Mackay sighting was reported to a local newspaper, the *Inverness Courier*, and as the saying goes, the rest is history. After the Mackay's, other people also began reporting what they'd seen in the loch, and this has continued over the years, right up until the present day.

Which brings us, I think, to the second part of my presentation today – some of the classic monster sightings. I would have to say that this photo is the image that most people think of when they hear the words Loch Ness monster. It was taken in 1934 by a London surgeon and has therefore come to be known as the surgeon's photograph. As you can see, it seems to show the head and neck of a strange animal sticking out of the water, and going by the ripples on the water surface, it appears that this was quite a large creature. Now, as I was just saying, this image is undoubtedly the most famous one around the world, but I'm afraid that in recent years, there's been some doubt about its authenticity. For example, in 1994, new evidence was uncovered which suggests that this photograph was in fact a complete hoax. Of course, we'll never probably know for sure, but now that there's been some negative evidence about this photo, it's unlikely that anyone will accept it as proof of a living creature ever again.

Another classic sighting that I'd like to share with you occurred in 1960. Tim Dinsdale, an aeronautical engineer, had gone to Loch Ness with the direct intention of trying to film the monster, and on the final day of his week-long expedition, he managed to see a large black hump. Dinsdale looked at this hump through binoculars and realized that he was watching a huge living creature, and at this point, he started filming it. The animal that Dinsdale filmed crossed the loch and started to submerge when it was quite near to the other side. After the film had been analyzed by experts from the RAF, the conclusion was that Dinsdale had indeed filmed, as they put it, 'an animate object', but it was impossible to say exactly what the object was. Over the years, people have criticized Dinsdale's film, saying that he must have filmed a boat, but of course these critics are conveniently forgetting that Dinsdale first examined the object through binoculars: if it had been a boat, then presumably he would easily have recognized it as such.

In the 1990s, the Dinsdale film was sent to America for further analysis and computer enhancement and they discovered some exciting features that hadn't been seen before. By computer enhancing the image of the hump, they found that there is actually a smaller hump right behind it. The debate around Dinsdale's film still continues to this day, but as I think you'll agree, the evidence does strongly suggest that he did in fact film exactly what he said he did: an unknown animal swimming in Loch Ness.

Time is marching on, so I'd like to move on to the final part of my presentation and consider the question: If there is a Loch Ness monster, what might it be?

As you probably know, a number of monster theories have been proposed over the years, although none of them are entirely satisfactory. One of the first theories, put forward in the very early days of the mystery, was that the monster might be a shark. Unfortunately, this theory failed to take into consideration the fact that Loch Ness is a freshwater lake, and of course sharks live in salt water. Needless to say, the shark hypothesis didn't last for long. Another early theory was that the monster might be an overgrown eel. The eel theory actually has quite a lot in its favour, but of course it doesn't explain everything. For example, witnesses typically report that the monster has a long neck like a giraffe, and none of the eels currently known to science are able to rise out of the water vertically and make a neck like that. So, unless we're dealing with a completely new species of eel, I'm afraid that this theory simply doesn't account for all the facts.

One of the most popular theories over the years has been that the monster is a type of marine dinosaur known as a plesiosaur. The skeletons that we have of plesiosaurs certainly look very similar to how the Loch Ness monster is usually described, but of course there are some major problems with this theory, not least the fact that dinosaurs such as the plesiosaur supposedly died out 70 million years ago. All things considered, I'd have to say that the plesiosaur theory is probably the least likely.

But I think I've said enough about what the monster *isn't* – at the start of this presentation, I promised that I would try to identify this creature or creatures, so let's now think about what the Loch Ness monster *is* …

If we go back to the very beginning of the mystery and look at some of the early reports from Loch Ness, we can see that the local people were talking about the monster simply being a large fish. And as unexciting as that might seem, this, in my opinion, is still the most likely candidate for the monster. One such fish, the Atlantic sturgeon, can grow very large indeed – specimens have been caught over three metres long – and because sturgeon are quite rare, most people would be unlikely to recognise them even if they saw one. A sturgeon living in the loch wouldn't need to feed on other fish – as you may know, one of the problems that scientists have always had with the concept of a monster is that there aren't really enough fish in Loch Ness to support any resident predators – and like a salmon, a sturgeon could simply come and go from the loch via one of the rivers. This would certainly help to account for the scarcity of sightings …

Now, I accept that the sturgeon theory can't account for every single sighting, but I personally think that back in the 1930s, a particularly large sturgeon was probably responsible for setting the whole thing off. As you may know, the waters of Loch Ness can be very deceptive – there are boat wakes; partially submerged rocks; floating tree trunks; and swimming deer … all sorts of confusing things – so once the idea of a monster was born, whenever people saw something that they couldn't easily explain in Loch Ness, they automatically thought of the monster. And of course, this has continued right up to the present day. In fact, I would say that it's now impossible for anyone to visit Loch Ness without associating it with the monster, in which case unexplained sightings – which I personally believe are simply cases of mistaken identity – are quite likely to continue.

So, that brings us to the end of my paper today. If anyone has any questions, I'll do my best to answer them …

Track 9: Speaking effectively: Intonation 1: Exercise 3.1

a) The surgeon's photograph was a hoax.
b) The surgeon's photograph was a hoax?

Track 10: Speaking effectively: Intonation 2: Exercise 3.2

a) Three quite common causes of monster sightings at Loch Ness are boat wakes, mirage effects and floating tree trunks.
b) Sonar readings have proved that the monster exists, haven't they?
c) Sonar readings can sometimes be false, can't they?
d) Why not use a submarine?
e) That brings us to the end of my presentation.

Track 11: Speaking effectively: Intonation 3: Exercise 3.4

a) The monster may just be a large fish.
b) It's possible that the witnesses were simply mistaken.

Track 12: Speaking effectively: Intonation 4: Exercise 3.6

a) The works of three authors have been particularly influential at Loch Ness: Rupert Gould, Constance Whyte and Tim Dinsdale.
b) The surgeon's photograph was exposed as a hoax in 1994, wasn't it?
c) Newspaper reports aren't always very reliable though, are they?
d) It may be that the monster feeds off the mud and sediment at the bottom of the loch.
e) Could the loch be drained?
f) It's possible that head and neck sightings are simply tree branches floating in the water.
g) Scientists last visited the loch in 2003.

Track 13: Answering questions 1: Exercise 4.1

S1: I have a question. Do you think the monster might be a large otter?
L: That's a very good question. It's certainly true that otters may have accounted for some of the sightings, particularly the ones on land. One night back in the 1930s….
S2: I still don't understand why the monster can't be a plesiosaur. Can you explain that part again?
L: Sorry. I didn't explain that very well. Let me try again. The main difficulty with the plesiosaur theory is that it's hard to see how such a creature could have got into the loch in the first place.
S3: So what do you mean when you said that unexplained sightings are simply cases of mistaken identities?
L: Let me try to put it another way. There are a number of factors at Loch Ness that make it particularly easy for people to get confused.

Track 14: Answering questions 2: Exercise 4.2

A1: That's a very good question. It's certainly true that otters may have accounted for some of the sightings, particularly the ones on land. One night back in the 1930s, two girls reported seeing a brown animal cross the road and enter the loch. Going on the girls' description, this was almost definitely just an otter.
A2: Sorry. I didn't explain that very well. Let me try again. The main difficulty with the plesiosaur theory is that it's hard to see how such a creature could have got into the loch in the

first place. At the time when the last known plesiosaurs became extinct, about 70 million years ago, Loch Ness didn't even exist – it was just a massive chunk of ice. The loch as we currently know it has only been around since the end of the Ice Age, so about 10,000 years ago. If we compare 70 million years and 10,000 years, the time gap is simply too big.

A3: Let me try to put it another way. There are a number of factors at Loch Ness that make it particularly easy for people to get confused. We know that under certain weather conditions, it's perfectly possible to see mirages at Loch Ness. This means that normal and easily identifiable objects such as water birds or floating tree trunks would seem much bigger. Boat wakes are another cause of confusion. For example, it's been observed that wakes on Loch Ness can appear as much as half an hour after the boat that caused them has disappeared.

Track 15: Closing phrases: Exercise 5.1

Closing 1
Does anyone have any more questions? In that case, I'll finish my presentation here. Thank you for listening.

Closing 2
If there are no more questions, I'll stop here. Thank you very much for your attention.

Unit 4
Track 16: Presentation openings: Exercise 1.1

Opening 1
Good morning, everyone. Before I start my presentation today, I'd like to ask you a question. How many of you here have eaten junk food in the last week? Could you put your hand up, please, if the answer is yes. Well, that's almost everyone. Now that's very interesting, because the topic of my presentation today is junk food and how it's contributing to teenage obesity.

Opening 2
Good morning, everyone. Before I start my presentation today, I'd like to share a few facts with you. As I'm sure you all know, here in Scotland, we have the highest mountain in the UK. And I'm also proud to say the largest freshwater lake. But let me tell you something that I'm not proud about. According to a recent survey, Scotland has the highest incidence of teenage obesity, not only in the UK, but in all of Europe. And in my presentation today, I'm going to be looking at junk food and how its consumption is contributing to the problem.

Opening 3
Good morning, everyone. Before we get started, I have a little task for you. Could you stand up, please, if you've had any junk food in the last week? Hmmm, that looks like more than half of you, which is very interesting, because the topic of my presentation today is junk food and how its consumption is contributing to teenage obesity.

Opening 4
Good morning, everyone. Before we get started, I'd like you to listen to something. It's a poem by the writer, Barbara Rice:

So many nights, I whimpered and cried,
Thought that my prayers had all been denied.
Stuffing my feelings, ashamed of my plight,
Trying to stop, with all of my might.
Shoving in cold spaghetti, at three in the morning,
Frying shrimps by the time the daylight was dawning.
Drinking gallons of soda, my heart wildly beating,
Hating myself, 'cause I couldn't stop eating.
The monster in me would come out to play,
And as much as I begged him, he wouldn't go away.
Morning would come, and that is when,
The whole vicious cycle would start once again …

The title of that poem is *Out of Hell: Reflections On Losing 150 Pounds*, and the topic of my presentation, if you haven't already guessed, is junk food and teenage obesity.

Track 17: Alternative openings: Exercise 2.0

Asking the audience a question
a) Before I start my presentation today, I'd like to ask you all a question. How many of you are married? Put your hand up, please, if your answer is yes.
b) Good afternoon, everyone. Before we get started, I have a quick question. Who was born before 1985? Please raise your hand if the answer is yes.

Asking the audience to do something
a) Before I start my presentation today, I'd like to carry out a little experiment. Can you stand up, please, if you've had any junk food in the last week?
b) Good morning, everyone. Before we get started, I have a little task for you. Can you stand up, please, if you've had any junk food in the last week?

Getting the audience's attention with some unexpected information
Good afternoon, everyone. Before I start my presentation today, I'd like to share a few facts with you. As you probably all know, Scotland has the highest mountain in the whole of the UK. You may also have heard that Scotland has the largest freshwater lake in the UK. But I wonder how many of you realize that, according to a recent survey, Scotland has the highest incidence of teenage obesity, not only in the UK, but in all of Europe.

Track 18: Word stress and meaning 1: Exercise 3.0

a) The situation isn't going to improve. The situation is not going to improve.
b) There wasn't any point in them doing that. There was no point in them doing that.
c) It's been a very difficult time. It has been a very difficult time.

Track 19: Word stress and meaning 2: Exercise 3.1

a) Global warming is not going to go away by itself.
b) We are trying to do something about it.
c) It has been difficult to convince people.
d) It is a worldwide issue.
e) We cannot ignore what the planet is telling us.
f) We are going to have to change our habits.

Track 20: Word stress and meaning 3: Exercise 4.3

a) It is highly unlikely to change.
b) The long-term effects of global warming are extremely worrying.
c) Doctors are becoming increasingly concerned about teenage obesity.
d) If the WHO receives more funding, the number of deaths can be dramatically reduced.

Track 21: Language for increasing the impact of presentations 1: Exercise 4.4

a) Global warming is a serious problem and one that demands our attention. The current climate is much, much milder than it used to be, and this is having a number of different effects.

b) One effect of global warming is that the warmer temperatures are causing the glaciers to melt. And from an environmental point of view, the implications of this are likely to be very, very serious indeed.

c) Another consequence of global warming is that we're noticing some significant changes in animal behaviour. Many, many animals are increasing their grazing range, and this is having a knock-on effect on all sorts of things.

Track 22: Language for increasing the impact of presentations 2: Exercise 4.5

a) Without doubt, the current situation is very, very serious.
b) If we received more funding, we could save many, many lives.
c) Our distribution networks are much, much better than they used to be.
d) It is far, far easier to prevent a problem from happening than to solve it later.

Track 23: Language for increasing the impact of presentations 3: Exercise 4.6

a) As I think you all know, more and more scientists are getting involved in climate research.

b) And of course, the good thing about this is that we're getting better and better at predicting what the long-term consequences of global warming are most likely to be.

c) But we still have the issue of how we should actually go about reducing greenhouse gas emissions. I think the root of the problem is that global warming affects almost every part of modern society. Take transportation, for example. We're all so dependant on cars, it's difficult to imagine our lives without them. And it's getting harder and harder to come up with affordable alternatives.

Track 24: Language for increasing the impact of presentations 4: Exercise 4.7

a) The temperature of the sea is getting warmer and warmer.
b) More and more people are becoming concerned.
c) Public opinion is growing stronger and stronger.
d) The weather is becoming less and less predictable.

Track 25: Achieving maximum impact when presenting numbers and data: Exercise 6.1

Pair 1
a) So far, 70 people have signed up for the scheme. Fifty-six of them have agreed to participate for at least six months.

b) So far, 70 people have signed up for the scheme. Fifty-six of them, in other words 80 per cent, have agreed to participate for at least six months.

Pair 2
a) According to one website, on an annual basis, extreme poverty claims the lives of 10,950,000 children.

b) According to one website, on an annual basis, extreme poverty claims the lives of 10,950,000 children. Just think about that. If you do the maths, it works out as 30,000 children every day.

Pair 3
a) Nutrition experts agree that most adults need a minimum of around 2,000 calories per day. When the Khmer Rouge were in power in Cambodia, workers in their labour camps were only given around 800 to 1,200.

b) Nutrition experts agree that most adults need around 2,000 calories per day. When the Khmer Rouge were in power in Cambodia, workers in their labour camps were only given around 800 to 1,200. That's between 40 and 60 per cent – about half the daily recommended allowance.

Unit 5
Track 26: Referring to visual aids 1: Exercise 6.1

Excerpt 1
As I mentioned earlier, this year we've seen a considerable increase in our international student memberships. Let's look at which countries these students are coming from and which clubs and societies they're choosing to join.

Excerpt 2
This graph represents the international students currently studying at the university. The vertical axis represents the number of students and the horizontal axis represents their country of origin. As you can see, most international students are coming from four key areas: China, Japan, Nigeria and India.

Excerpt 3
As the graph shows, the university Travel Club is still the most popular society for international students, particularly for students from China and Nigeria. But I would also draw your attention to two other societies: the student Debating Group and the Drama Circle. As the data here indicates, the student Debating Group is a popular choice with Indian students, and the Drama Circle attracts lots of members from Japan.

Track 27: Referring to visual aids 2: Exercise 6.3

Excerpt 4
So now let's look at how international students spend their leisure time. This table provides an overview of 200 students from Newtown College in 2007.

As you can see, the first column, the column on the left, shows the students' country of origin, and then the six columns on the right provide details of their different leisure activities. The points in bold represent the most popular activities for each ethnic group.

As this data shows, playing computer games was rated as the most popular leisure activity for Chinese students. For the Japanese, on the other hand, the most popular activity was shopping. The Nigerians said that they liked playing sports best, and finally, the Indian students responded that their favourite leisure-time activity was meeting friends.

Track 28: Connected speech 1: Exercise 7.1

a) We should have started recruiting in Asia much earlier.
b) One of the new doctorate students arrived last week.

c) He came with his wife and kids.
d) Have you met him yet?

Track 29: Connected speech 2: Exercise 7.2

a) He's an actor.
b) He's coming next week.
c) That was the last time I saw him.
d) She isn't one of my students. [pause] He went to unload his car. [pause] Australia is warmer than Britain.

Track 30: Connected speech 3: Exercise 7.3

a) She needs to ask his permission.
b) He was an officer in the army.
c) Just stay there for a moment.
d) It's a bit tight.

Unit 6
Track 31: Persuasive vs informative openings: Exercise 3.1

Opening 1

Good morning, everyone. As you know, my name is Peter Barker and I'm a student here at New College. In my presentation today, I'm going to talk about cycling to the campus rather than coming by car. Basically, my presentation will be in three parts. In the first part, I'll talk about some environmental issues. Then I'll look at the financial side of things, and to finish off, I'll focus on personal safety.

Opening 2

Good morning, everyone. As you know, my name's Richard McGarry and I'm a student here at New College. In my presentation today, I'm going to focus on why I strongly believe that more people should be cycling to the campus rather than coming by car. Basically, my presentation will be in three parts. In the first part, I'll show you the environmental benefits of leaving the car at home. Then, I'll let you see just how much money you could save. And to finish off, I'll demonstrate how travelling to the campus by bicycle can have a massive impact on everyone's personal safety.

Track 32: Persuasive vs informative conclusions: Exercise 3.2

Conclusion 1

That brings us to the end of my presentation today. Thank you very much for listening. If anyone has any questions, I'd be happy to answer them.

Conclusion 2

That brings us to the end of my presentation today. As I'm sure you'll now agree, travelling to the campus by bicycle can offer you a number of distinct advantages, not only in terms of helping the environment, but also in terms of saving you money and raising the level of your personal safety. Thank you very much for listening. If anyone has any questions, I'd be happy to answer them.

Track 33: Giving reasons and building arguments: Exercises 4.1 and 4.2

Arming the police would only lead to increased levels of violence on our streets. Aside from the fact that if all our policemen started carrying guns, then all our criminals would too, there'd also be a much greater risk of innocent people getting hurt. In most inner city shoot-outs, it's neither the police nor the criminals that end up getting shot – it's innocent passers-by like you and me.

But I'm sure some of you are still thinking, if the police carried guns, then wouldn't it work as a deterrent to violent crime? Well, all the evidence from countries where police carry the guns on a daily basis shows that the violent crime rate actually goes up, not down. And of course, America is a prime example of this …

Review unit
Track 34: Review exercise: Exercise 1.1

Good morning, everyone, I think we'd better get started. My name is Dr Steven Bishop. Thank you very much for coming along to my presentation today. Now, for the next ten minutes or so, I'm going to talk about a substance that we're all very familiar with and one that none of us can do without. Have you any idea as to what that might be?
[Q from the audience: Are you going to talk about food?]
No, it's not food, but you're thinking along the right lines. Anyone else, perhaps?
[Q from the audience: Is it something that we drink? Is it water?]
Yes, of course. What could be more important than water? Basically, I'm going to talk about the chemical substance H_2O, better known as water … and to highlight the importance of this substance, the presentation is entitled 'Water: The Amazing Liquid of Life'.

Now, I've divided my presentation into three parts. And to start, I'm going to talk about where water comes from and where the Earth keeps most of its current reserves. Then, I'd like to focus on what I'll call 'the wonders of water' and give you some interesting facts about its physical properties. And to finish off, I'll say a little about some of the key features of our great oceans and seas.

So let's start, then, with where water comes from; its early history, if you like.

Track 35: Review Exercise: Exercise 1.2

Now, the first point I'd like to make is that the Earth retains all of the water ever created – an amount that some scientists have estimated as a massive 326 million cubic miles – so when we're talking about water, it's important to remember that we're referring to a substance that has been used, purified and then reused for about 3,000 million years.

But where did it all come from in the first place? Well, the accepted scientific theory of how water was first created states that when the Earth was formed, a chemical reaction took place between the gases hydrogen and oxygen. As you know, the chemical name for water is H_2O, which is two parts hydrogen, one part oxygen. So basically, the way it worked is that these gases, hydrogen and oxygen, were in the atmosphere, circling the newly-formed Earth, and as they reacted together, they became liquid particles and formed a dense layer of cloud. And as the temperatures dropped, this layer of cloud released its water in a torrential downpour that lasted an amazing 60,000 years. This filled the lower land basins, forming the oceans and seas as we know them today. And you know, the truly remarkable thing is, the level of the oceans and the amount of water on the Earth has actually remained relatively stable ever since.

Now, if we think about our water reserves and where our water is actually based, as you might expect, the bulk of the Earth's water, about 97.2 per cent of it, lies in the great oceans. 2.15 per cent is held in ice caps and glaciers, and the remainder is spread out in an area ranging from three miles below the Earth's surface to seven miles up in the atmosphere. Some of you might think that rivers and streams are a key storage place for the Earth's water, but in fact, these only account for 0.0001 per cent, about 300 cubic miles. The other surface water totals around 55,000 cubic miles and can be divided up between inland seas and fresh and saltwater lakes.

Apart from its surface water, the Earth has a reserve supply of some 200,000 cubic miles of water below the surface. The water in the upper layer, known as the aeration zone, clings to the soil and rocks and is either absorbed by plants or returns to the air through evaporation. Other water supplies can be found deeper in what is known as the saturation zone. The water here feeds swamps, rivers, lakes and wells, and it can turn up in the most unlikely places. For example, I'm sure you'll be surprised to hear that the Sahara Desert has an underground reservoir of about 150,000 cubic miles.

Moving back above ground, the atmosphere holds about 3,100 cubic miles of water – enough to cover the entire planet with one inch of rain if it all came down at the same time. In actual fact, this atmospheric water does eventually fall as rain and is replaced by evaporation every 12 days or so. And despite what the nursery rhyme says about 'the rain in Spain falling mainly on the plain', most of our rainfall actually ends up in the seas and rivers. Only about ⅙ of the planet's total rainfall soaks into the ground.

Now I'd like to move onto the second part of my presentation today, and look at some of water's wonders. As a substance, water has a number of unique properties, one of the most interesting ones being the fact that when it meets other materials, it forms a skin. You see, water molecules are more strongly attracted to themselves than to other substances and as a result, they squeeze together, forming a dense layer. This phenomenon is called surface tension, and sometimes you can actually see it in action. For example, you may have noticed that insects have this almost magical ability to walk on water – well, that comes down to water's surface tension.

Another one of water's strange properties is that it can absorb more heat than almost any other common substance, without it experiencing a considerable rise in temperature. For example, when a kettle of water is put on to boil, it is subjected to a temperature that would cause most other substances to either melt or burst into flames. But in the case of water, it just soaks up the heat until a temperature of 100 degrees centigrade is reached. And as we all know, at this point, water boils and we can see the steam bubbles bursting through its surface tension.

So that's what happens when water gets hot, but what about when it gets cold? Well, another one of water's wonders is that it floats when frozen. This is because water expands at freezing point and becomes less dense. As we know, in the Arctic regions, huge ice floes cover the surfaces of lakes and oceans and basically, these act as a protective, insulating blanket. The ice floes prevent further freezing and help life go on underneath the blanket of ice. So you see, the fact that frozen water floats is very important for the survival of both us and our planet, because

if it didn't, the ice would gradually build up from the ocean beds and cover the entire Earth in a solid glacier-like mass. And needless to say, if that happened, life as we currently know it would simply not be able to survive.

This brings us to the final part of my presentation today. And as promised at the beginning, to finish off, I'd like to say a little about our great oceans and seas.

When you look out over an ocean or a sea, if you were actually able to see beneath the waves, you'd find a whole new world of spectacular canyons, great plains and enormous mountain ranges. One such mountain range, the Mid-Atlantic Ridge, runs for about 10,000 miles between Iceland and the Antarctic, which makes it the largest mountain range in the world. And in fact, believe it or not, Iceland, the Ascension Islands and the Azores are just all examples of this underwater mountain range's highest peaks.

Now, as well as great mountain ranges, our oceans also hide some extremely deep holes and trenches. The deepest known trench is the so-called 'Challenger Deep', situated off the island of Guam in the Pacific. This trench goes down for an amazing seven miles, and just to give you some idea of how deep that actually is, if we were to put Everest into it, there would still be about a mile of water above the summit. Surprising, isn't it?

Now, as I said a moment ago, our oceans contain spectacular canyons. The Hudson Canyon, just off the coast of New York, is 150 miles long and 16,500 feet deep. The creatures living at the bottom of this canyon have to be able to cope with *tremendous* water pressure. And just to give you some idea of what I mean by that, at a depth of 13,000 feet, the water pressure is nearly three tons to the square foot, so if we're looking at a depth of over 16,000 feet, clearly only highly specialized organisms are able to survive; most animals would actually find such living conditions intolerable.

The last information I'd like to share with you about the oceans and seas is with regard to their currents and tides. As you've probably heard, one of the most powerful ocean currents is known as the Gulf Stream. When this current leaves the Caribbean, it's about 50 miles wide and up to 1,500 feet deep, and it flows across the Atlantic at a speed of about five knots, which in terrestrial terms is equal to almost six miles per hour. As for tides, well, as every schoolchild knows, the daily rise and fall of tides is caused by the gravitational pull of the moon and the sun. The effect of each pull causes, in effect, a bulge in the ocean. Our large tides – the Spring tides – occur when the sun and moon are pulling on the same side of the Earth; when the sun and the moon pull at right angles, we get Neap tides, which are the smallest. The largest tides of all occur in places where the sea runs into bottlenecks, such as in the Bay of Fundy on America's east coast. And this makes for some truly spectacular viewing.

Well, that pretty much brings me to the end of my presentation today. I've talked about a very common subject, water, but as I hope to have shown, H_2O is truly our planet's 'amazing liquid of life'.

Now, if anyone has any questions, I'll do my best to answer them.

Track 36: Review exercise: Exercise 1.4

[FADE IN] Well, that pretty much brings me to the end of my presentation today. I've talked about a very common subject, water, but as I hope to have shown, H_2O is truly our planet's 'amazing liquid of life'.

Now, if anyone has any questions, I'll do my best to answer them.

Q1: I have a question. In your presentation, you said that the Earth retains all of the water ever created. Do you mean to say that no new water is ever produced?

A: Well, that's a good question, and to answer it … (fade out)

Q2: In your presentation, you said that the oceans were created by a downpour that lasted for 60,000 years. How exactly do we know that?

A: OK, let me explain. For one thing, when we … (fade out)

Q3: I'm still not sure about how surface tension works. Can you go over that part again?

A: Well, I'm sorry if that wasn't very clear. You know what I was saying about insects,… (fade out)

Track 37: Review exercise: Exercise 2.6

a) So let's start, then, with where water comes from; its early history, if you like.
b) Now, the first point I'd like to make is that the Earth retains all of the water ever created.
c) The accepted scientific theory of how water was first created states that when the Earth was formed, a chemical reaction took place between the gases hydrogen and oxygen.
d) As the temperatures dropped, this layer of cloud released its water in a torrential downpour that lasted an amazing 60,000 years.
e) The truly remarkable thing is, the level of the oceans and the amount of water on the Earth has actually remained relatively stable ever since.

Track 38: Review exercise: Exercise 2.7

f) The Earth's surface water is stored in rivers, lakes, oceans and seas.
g) Water floats when it's frozen, doesn't it?
h) Of course, water floats when it's frozen, doesn't it? That's why we have icebergs.
i) This brings us to the final part of my presentation.
j) Does anyone have any questions?

Track 39: Review exercise: Exercise 2.9

a) Water in the saturation zone feeds swamps, rivers, lakes and wells.
b) When water boils, we can see bubbles bursting through the surface tension, can't we? That's the point when we know its temperature has reached 100 degrees.
c) Are the ice floes really that important?
d) The largest tides occur in places where the sea runs into bottlenecks.

Track 40: Review exercise: Exercise 2.10

a) The truly remarkable thing is that the level of the oceans has actually remained relatively stable ever since.
b) Most animals would find such living conditions absolutely intolerable.
c) If the ice built up from the ocean beds, life as we currently know it would be completely unable to survive.
d) Without surface tension, it would be totally impossible for insects to walk on water.

Track 41: Review exercise: Exercise 2.11

e) There can be no doubt whatsoever that water is a very, very important substance.
f) There are many, many cubic miles of water hidden beneath the Earth's surface.
g) It is far, far easier for us to waste water than it is to save it.
h) As you go deeper, the water pressure becomes greater and greater.
i) Once you get past a few thousand feet, it becomes harder and harder for organisms to survive unless they're highly specialized.

Track 42: Review exercise: Exercise 3.5

As this diagram shows, the hydrologic cycle, commonly known as the 'water cycle', consists of seven major processes. As you can see on the left, the first of these two processes happen at about the same time and are known as EVAPORATION and TRANSPIRATION. Basically, evaporation refers to the process when surface water is converted into water vapour, whereas transpiration refers to the evaporation of water from plants. The third process is called CONDENSATION – this happens when the rising water vapour cools and is converted back into liquid water in the form of clouds. These clouds are then transported across the sky by the wind and eventually, this leads to the fourth main process in the cycle, PRECIPITATION, which refers to the cloud water falling back to the Earth in the form of rain, sleet, hail or snow. Once it's back on the Earth, the water moves into process five, INFILTRATION, which refers to the water draining back into the surface soil. The water then works its way down through these upper layers of soil, a process known as PERCOLATION, to join the groundwater already stored under the surface. This then leads to the final stage of the cycle, a process known as RUNOFF. Runoff refers to the movement of ground and surface water back to the main body of water, such as rivers, lakes or seas, from which the whole cycle begins again.